Luck of the Draw

LUCK OF THE DRAW

TRUE-LIFE TALES OF LOTTERY WINNERS AND LOSERS

Chris Gudgeon & Barbara Stewart

ARSENAL PULP PRESS
Vancouver

ARSENAL PULP PRESS
103-1014 Homer Street
Vancouver, B.C.
Canada V6B 2W9
www.arsenalpulp.com

The publisher gratefully acknowledges the support of the Canada Council for the Arts and the B.C. Arts Council for its publishing program, and the support of the Government of Canada through the Book Publishing Industry Development Program for its publishing activities.

An earlier version of *Luck of the Draw* was published by Prentice Hall Canada in 1995.

Typeset by Robert Ballantyne
Printed and bound in Canada

CANADIAN CATALOGUING IN PUBLICATION DATA:
Gudgeon, Chris, 1959-
Luck of the draw

ISBN 1-55152-082-6

1. Lottery winners—Canada. 2. Lotteries—Canada.
3. Lottery winners—United States. 4. Lotteries—United States.
5. Stewart, Barbara, 1960- II. Title.
HG6147.G84 2001   795.3'8'0922   C00-911004-6

CONTENTS

Acknowledgments

Many thanks to:

The winners, losers, and players who shared their lottery stories.

The people at state and provincial lottery corporations and at other private institutions, who offered their help.

The people at Prentice Hall, original publishers of the book, and Arsenal Pulp Press, particularly Brian, Blaine, and Robert, for all their hard work.

Our friend, Daphne Hart.

To Charlie, Tavish, and Keating, who prove that miracles happen.

In loving memory of Jan Senyk and Gertrude Oliver.

INTRODUCTION

"No one needs that much money."
—Lillian Kelly, on winning a $13.9 million Lotto 6/49 jackpot

Money. Gobs of it. Everyone dreams about it—almost no one can ever get enough of it. It doesn't grow on trees—surely your mother told you that—but sometimes, if you're lucky, it appears as if by magic. . . .

The magic of the lottery, that is, which in an instant can transform a legal secretary or unemployed father or dock worker or waitress or bank manager into a multimillionaire. The lottery is the only reliable miracle left in this age of reason; no matter what else happens this week, you can be sure that someone, somewhere, will win it big.

It's an international obsession. Each week in North America alone, we spend almost half a billion dollars on lotteries and other state-run gambling schemes. Every year, seven out of ten adults buy at least one lottery ticket, while every state and province in North America runs at least half a dozen lottery schemes, from lotto draws to scratch-and-wins, to bingo games and, increasingly, casinos. Pretty remarkable considering that thirty years ago lotteries were illegal and held in contempt by upright people. Such "numbers games," it was said, were the domain of organized criminals, who preyed on the gullible and disadvantaged.

But beneath our lottery fantasies lurk nagging doubts about the personal, emotional, and social costs. "I'd hate to win a million," a cab driver in Montreal told us. "You lose your friends, your family, and you'd be afraid to walk the streets for fear someone would kill you just for your wallet." Despite his concerns, though, he shrugged and admitted that he never missed a draw.

This is the story of lotteries. It's told through the eyes and words of ordinary people. Many of them are winners who reveal the personal stories behind the headlines, but some are losers who offer a note of caution. The Lottery gods, it seems, have a keen sense of irony, and one can never be sure exactly what they have in store. This book also contains lots of practical advice on how to play lotteries, and on what to do with your millions when you win.

Chance. Destiny. Fluke. Karma. It's the Luck Of The Draw, and when it happens, dreams are made—and sometimes, nightmares begin.

CHAPTER 1

THE SUMMER OF LOTTO LOVE

"You go from totally excited to scared to death."
—Record Powerball jackpot co-winner John Jarell

Maybe it was the heat. Something was certainly in the air the summer of 1998.

At first, there seemed to be nothing more than the usual interest in Des Moines-based Multi State Lottery Association's July 29 Powerball draw. Less than a week before, the jackpot had flirted with the $100 million mark, but ticket sales were off some thirty percent and the hype didn't come close to the frenzy that preceded the May 20 draw, when people lined up for hours on a chance for a record $195 million prize pool.

Perhaps there was a prevailing sense of lunchbag letdown. The week following the record win, the jackpot reached a mere $10 million. Powerball sales declined dramatically, and no one seemed to care when the draw came and went without a winner. Could it be that in a country inundated with media messages—where 80 percent of the adult population gambled at least once in a while, and where lotteries alone were a $40 billion business—a $200 million jackpot just didn't grab the public's attention any more? The MUSL, an amalgamation of twenty states and the District of Columbia, had seen sales lulls before. But as draw after draw passed without a winner—nineteen in all—lottery organizers watched the prize pool grow without sparking the kind of lotto-buying lunacy they'd come to expect.

CANUCK LUCK: LOTTOMANIA

 Canadians experienced their own Summer of Lotto Love in 1984, a time when it seemed the whole country had gone stark raving lotto-crazy. A new word entered the vocabulary: "Lottomania."

The seeds of lottomania were planted late in 1983. Nobody won the jackpot on the year's final Lotto 6/49, a national lottery, and by the time of the first draw in the New Year the big prize was up to $7 million. In the week leading up to it, 11 million Canadians spent an unprecedented $67 million on tickets, and the jackpot increased to close to $14 million. People lined up for as long as three hours as computers strained to keep up with the demand. Meanwhile, Americans were crossing the border in droves to buy a ticket on this chance of a lifetime, only to have their dreams dashed by customs officials on their way back home: a 50-year-old law forbade anyone from transporting lottery tickets onto U.S. soil.

As the January 14 draw date drew closer, Lotto 6/49 became front page news. Church groups complained about the erosion of the work ethic; government officials called for a jackpot cap to discourage future lotto frenzies; financial planners doled out tax advice to potential instant millionaires, while past winners implored the next members of their fraternity to get unlisted phone numbers and lay low.

On January 14, millions of Canadians tuned into CTV's live broadcast to find out if fortune would smile on them. Host Tom Gibney, a well-known Toronto newscaster, read the numbers on the rubber balls as they fired out of the draw machine—2, 12, 29, 31, 44, and 46. In a matter of seconds, it was over. A computer check indicated that one lucky player in central Ontario was now $13,890,588.80 richer. But in the days that followed, no one came forward to claim the prize. As each day passed, 6/49 officials feared that something had gone seriously wrong. Maybe the ticket had been lost or stolen? Maybe someone had stuck it in a drawer and forgot about it? Or maybe it was bought by an American and confiscated at the border? Lottery officials feared that the lack of a winner

But all at once something clicked and it seemed that everyone caught the fever. Three-hour line-ups were the norm at many of the 45,000 ticket outlets, and in towns that bordered states that weren't part of the MUSL, some line-ups were running ten hours or longer. Extra police and security guards were brought in to keep the peace, while the urban myth machine worked could create an embarrassing situation; some people would undoubtedly suspect that the whole thing was rigged.

On Friday, January 20, Lillian Kelly, 54, quit her $150-a week part-time job at the Speed Queen laundry in Brantford, one hour west of Toronto. That same day, her husband Stuart applied for early retirement from Thibodeau-Finch Express, the trucking firm where he'd worked for 35 years. Stuart, 57, a $400-a-week driver, was already on disability leave, recovering from hip surgery.

Like most Canadians, Lillian had watched the Lotto 6/49 draw six nights earlier, and had jotted down the winning numbers in the margin of her *TV Guide* as they were announced. A few minutes later, she went to the kitchen and checked the first four tickets. She couldn't have expected much. The Kellys had been spending $10 a week on tickets since the lotteries began; the most they'd ever won was $100. But when she looked at the first number of the next ticket, her heart almost stopped. She had the winner.

The Kellys spent a sleepless night worrying about the ticket's hiding place (the sweater drawer, although the next day, they moved it to a safety deposit box), and what adverse effects the money might have on their health and lifestyle. They prayed that other winners would come forward and share in their windfall. By the next day it was clear that they held the only winning ticket. They contacted their lawyer, and paid a visit to their family doctor to make sure that their systems could handle a $14 million shock.

Two days after finally announcing their win to the world, the Kellys went into hiding. They were never happy about being the centre of media attention, and in the back of their minds, feared for their safety. Sadly, Stuart Kelly did not live long enough to enjoy his wealth. Six months after his record win, he died. The official cause was cancer, but some people couldn't help but wonder if the strain of winning didn't have something to do with his death, and that maybe Stuart Kelly had become another victim of the luck of the draw.

overtime: a woman in Arizona, it was said, gave birth to twins as she waited in line to buy $200 worth of tickets; an elderly man in Greenwich, Connecticut—because of its close proximity to New York City, scene of some of the longest line-ups in the country—died waiting for his chance, his wife refusing to leave the queue until her husband's last act had been fulfilled.

Meanwhile, at Canada-U.S. border crossings, traffic was backed up for miles as those crazy Canucks, members of perhaps the most lotto-mad nation on earth, made pilgrimages to the nearest Powerball mecca. Powerball had a special power for Canadians: by the day of the draw, the jackpot had risen to almost $300 million, which, when converted, worked out to almost $450 million Canadian. That's a lot of back bacon and beer.

As the July 29 draw deadline neared it was clear that it wasn't just the summer's heat driving people crazy: the lure of winning the big one had taken over. In four days, North Americans bought 150 million Powerball tickets, at a rate of 20,000 tickets a minute in the waning hours of the frenzy. One retailer in Connecticut reported selling more than 25,000 tickets a day, more—much more—than they'd expect to sell in a single week. And their take for all that hard work? At five cents per ticket, it worked out to $1,250—nothing to sneeze at, but hardly worth all the headaches. In fact, most vendors look at lottery tickets as a kind of loss leader, a high-maintenance low-profit item that helps to bring customers in the doors. There can be a silver lining, though; the store that sold the winning ticket was in line for its own windfall: a $100,000 bonus from the good folks at MUSL.

Finally, the moment of truth had arrived. At exactly 9:52 on Wednesday evening, the computerized ticket dispensers shut down. Although the final tally wouldn't be in for another day, the final sales total stood at $295.7 million. While it wasn't the world record the PR people at MUSL claimed—Spain's famous El Gordo lottery regularly tops the billion-dollar mark—it was a healthy chunk of change and the biggest prize pool American lottery players had ever seen. With the draw only minutes away, the country held its collective breath.

What was this strange game and how did it come to outdraw almost every other lottery on the planet? The roots of Powerball go back to September 1987, when five states banded together to form the Multi-State Lottery Company. Overshadowed by more lucrative jackpots offered by big states like California and New York, the members of MUSL—Iowa, Kansas, Oregon, Rhode Island, and West Virginia, along with the District of Columbia—hoped to find strength, or at least safety, in numbers. Within the month, Missouri jumped on board and the MUSL was ready to launch its first game. It was called Lotto America, probably because a lot o' America couldn't have cared less about it: in its first six months, Lotto America had sales of around $32 million, chump change when you consider that the profits had to be split eight ways.

The following year, MUSL upped the ante, switching from a 7/40 style game (where winners had to pick seven correct numbers from one to 40) to a 6/54 game (six correct numbers out of 54). This made the game a little harder to win but also meant that the average jackpot would be bigger, and in the lottery game nothing succeeds like excess. Big jackpots mean big sales. The strategy was moderately successful, and by 1991 MUSL was enjoying annual sales of more than $400 million. But by now Wisconsin, Montana, Idaho, Indiana, Delaware, Kentucky, South Dakota, Maine, and Minnesota had joined in. There were a lot more potential players, but overhead was up accordingly as each member state's percentage split was down: the average take was under $12 million per state.

Still, MUSL had learned its lesson; players wanted low stakes games with big payoffs. In April 1992, the state-run corporation introduced its new baby: Powerball. In the beginning, it was a 5/45 + 1/45 game, meaning that winners had to pick five correct numbers out of a pool of 45 as well as one "powerball" number out of a pool of 45. Odds were listed at 55 million-to-one. Predictably, jackpots and sales increased, but after three years of record-breaking sales, Powerball took a U-turn south. Sales in 1997 reached just under $900 million, a drop of $300 million from the previous year. Part of the problem was that the state of Georgia, which had joined the lotto union in 1995, decided to drop out on moral grounds. The strong fundamentalist movement had persuaded the state legislature that lotteries were no way for a state to earn a living. But Powerball was also facing stiffer competition from other state lotteries as well as a range of other legal gambling options—from casinos to video lottery terminals

THE SPANISH WIN CONDITION

 Powerball officials regularly claim that their jackpots are the largest in history. But even the largest prize pool pales in comparison to Spain's *El Gordo*, "the fat one." Lottery-mad Spaniards have made this annual Christmas Eve lottery a multi-billion dollar extravaganza.

Even in a country where every man, woman, and child spends an average of $850 a year on lotteries, *El Gordo* stands out. In 1997, for example, Spaniards spent $81.7 billion on lottery tickets. While there are thousands of prizes, the top ticket-holder took home an $85 million prize check—a nice little Christmas present.

Of course, a game so big is not without its strange side, like the group who split a $42 third-prize ticket in the late-1980s. All of them were members of an army unit . . . that had once tried to overthrow the government.

to sports betting—which were starting to emerge. On top of everything else, five more states—New England, Louisiana, Connecticut, New Hampshire, and New Mexico—had joined MUSL, which meant a further split of the profit. Something had to give.

That something came in the form of a kinder but not gentler Powerball. Launched in November 1997, the new game now featured a 5/49 +1/42 format. The changes seem slight, but looks can be deceiving. The first part is relatively easy: the odds of getting five out of 49 numbers are a mere 1,906,684 to one, on a par with your chance of being killed falling out of bed. It's that damn red powerball that causes all the trouble; increasing the odds 42 times to a rather startling 80,089,128 to one; much better than your chance of being killed by a falling meteor, but significantly worse—42 times worse, in fact—than the odds of being struck by lightning. Ouch. Again, the strategy was to build up the prize pool. Officials from MUSL confidently predicted that within the year they'd see a $100 million jackpot; in fact, they had two in the first two months. Annual sales jumped back over the 1 billion mark and have stayed there ever since.

At 10:59 p.m. on Wednesday, July 29, the two Beietel Criterion drawing machines at the MUSL's Des Moines headquarters whirled into action. One by one in numeric order, a lottery official fed 49 white high-density

---

BIG GAME HUNTERS

 The Lucky 13's big win made headlines across North America, but it's not the biggest lottery win in history. In fact, Powerball has relinquished its record-jackpot crown to Michigan's Big Game. In May, 2000, two ticket holders split a $363 million Big Game jackpot—a world record for a single winning number in a lottery. Meanwhile, Maria Grasso took home a $197 million prize in an April 1999 draw. Mere pocket change, really, but enough to qualify her for the biggest unshared lottery win in history.

---

rubber balls, each slightly bigger than a golf ball, into one of the machines; the process was repeated in the other machine with 42 red Powerballs. The balls bounced around the drum for five seconds, then as the process slowed down, a hole opened up in the bottom of one drum. The lottery machine spat out the first white ball: number 43. Four more balls followed in quick succession: 8, 39, 45, 49. A moment later, the official opened the release at the bottom of the second machine. There was a pause before the ball rolled out: lucky number 13.

As the numbers were read out and transmitted to broadcast outlets across the country, you could almost feel the ground shift with the collective weight of several hundred million fallen expectations. Still, there were a lot of happy players. By design, Powerball combines two kinds of lottery games, which helps to spread the winnings around. On the one hand, Powerball offers a jackpot game, where a portion of all the money bet—roughly 29 percent—goes to a cash prize for people holding all six winning numbers. Meanwhile, there's also a set cash prize of $100,000 for anyone holding all five numbers on the 5/49 portion of the game, not to mention a three-dollar tip for anyone getting the right Powerball number. That means that, theoretically at least, there's no limit to the amount of money the MUSL could pay out in any given lottery. While statistically, the MUSL could expect to pony up ten $100,000 prizes each draw, that number frequently goes much higher. On July 29, when all was said and done, 79 players were five-ball winners, and another three million players had tripled their original one-dollar investment. And somewhere, someone or some group of someones held the single winning lottery ticket.

One of the people not watching the draw that night was John Jarrell of Parkridge, just outside of Columbus, Ohio. Convinced that the odds were not on his side, Jarrell had gone to bed, leaving a pile of Powerball tickets with his wife. For six years, Jarrell and his co-workers at Automation Tooling Systems in nearby Westerville had been pooling their money to buy tickets on the state lottery and every once in a while, when a big jackpot came along, they'd take a chance on that too. The giant Powerball jackpot was irresistible. Everyone in their group chipped in ten dollars to buy 130 tickets. John almost balked; things were tight, and ten bucks was twice what he already put out each week on the Ohio lottery. But finally, he joined in. A couple guys jumped in the car and drove to their favourite Powerball outlet, Speedway, 100 miles away in Richmond, Indiana.

Jarrell's wife Sandy watched the live broadcast of the Powerball draw, writing the numbers on a piece of paper. Then she compared the list with a stack of photocopied tickets. All of a sudden, her heart jumped. She ran to the bedroom, screaming for her husband to turn on the light.

He looked at the numbers. "We've got it," he told his wife. He waved the winning ticket—his ticket—to the biggest lottery jackpot in American history.

TOP TEN POWERBALL JACKPOTS

1. $295,7000,932	July 29, 1998	The Lucky 13, Columbus, Ohio
2. $194,462,540	May 20, 1998	Frank & Shirley Capaci, Illinois
3. $151,000,000	June 30, 1999	Farrah Slad, Minnesota
4. $150,193,741	March 4, 2000	26 airline workers, Oklahoma Keith & Carol Gorgen, Minnestoa Gary & Beverly Ruff, Missouri
5. $111,240,463	July 7, 1993	Leslie Robbins & Colleen DeVries, Wisconsin
6. $101,844,679	March 4, 1995	Don & Shirley Pence, Arizona
7. $101,043,086	Nov. 30, 1994	Gary Allen, Indiana Connie Daily, Nebraska
8. $ 89,533,943	Dec. 22, 1993	Percy R. Pridgen, Washington, D.C.
9. $ 89,366,297	Jan. 24, 1996	Kent Miller, Tennessee
10. $ 87,585,067	June 3, 1995	Pam Hiatt, Idaho

The Jarrell's spent the rest of the night on the phone calling co-workers, friends, and relatives. By morning, they had a plan. They left the ticket in a safety deposit box—because it had to be redeemed in the state where it was bought, the ticket would later make the journey back to Indiana by armoured car—and John Jarrell met up with his 12 co-winners at work the next day. It was pandemonium: everyone was hugging and laughing and crying and giving high fives and slapping each other on the back. Even Robert Kronk was happy. Kronk wasn't one of the lucky thirteen, but if it hadn't been for a strange quirk of fate it could have been a different story. Kronk had been part of the lottery pool for years, but three months before the big draw he decided to drop out. He was tired of playing the quick pick—letting the computer select a random set of numbers—and wanted to take matters into his own hands. Big mistake.

At the end of the day, all that was left was for Jarrell and his partners to collect their winnings. But it wasn't as simple as that. First they had to decide: one lump or 25? See, Powerball gave them the option of taking the full jackpot amount in 25 equal annual payments or a one-time, lump sum buyout. These buyouts were always much less than the advertised jackpots, but in the long run, if properly invested, could prove much more lucrative. Ultimately, the Lucky 13 opted for a $161.5 million buyout which meant that, after taxes, each partner would take home roughly $6.8 million. And even though that figure was a far cry from the $297.5 million dreams of Powerball's frenzied fans, it did nothing to dim the success of the Summer of Lottery Love. It was perhaps the lottery's finest moment in this country, and proof that the luck of the draw had taken hold of our collective consciousness.

CHAPTER 2

BACK TO THE FUTURE

Lotteries have been around forever. Some say that the Great Wall of China was built with money raised by lottery, and that no Roman party was complete without an after-dinner draw, with prizes ranging from gold coins to dead flies and live ostriches.

The roots of the modern lottery can be found during the Renaissance. The first commercial lottery was in the French town of L'Esluse, in 1420, with the proceeds going towards moat improvements and the like. In Venice in the 1520s, an enterprising used-clothing salesman named Geronimo Bambarara came up with the idea of selling merchandise by lot. He started off small, selling chances for 20 *soldi*, the lowest form of currency, but within a few weeks this backdoor lottery was all the rage, and prices went through the roof. It was the Powerball of its day, attracting crowds happy to stand in line for hours for a chance to win a parcel of silk, gold ducats, a horse, and on one occasion, even a wild cat.

It didn't take long for the government to notice what was going on. At first, Venetian authorities tried to control lotteries in order to protect their citizens. Lotteries had to be sanctioned by the courts and fraud was harshly punished; no one could rob a Venetian blind and get away with it. Soon, though, the government realized it was sitting on a cash cow. Even those most opposed to taxation seemed happy for the chance to lose a few lira in even the lamest lottery game.

While the Venetians came up with the concept of state-run lotteries as a revenue resource, it was up to their cousins in Genoa to refine the

THE LUCK OF THE IRISH

 Most people over the age of 50 remember the Irish Sweepstakes. In the days before legal lotteries, the Sweeps was the only game in town. Sure, it was illegal, but the money went to a good cause—the Hospital Trust Fund, in Dublin—and it was damn fun to play.

The Sweepstakes began in 1930 when the fledgling Irish Free State was desperate for cash. The government authorized a "sweepstakes," a kind of horse-race-based lottery. Here's how it worked: North Americans bought their tickets through the mail or from some backroom distributor—the Sweeps had a certain underworld flavor that added to its charm—then, a handful of tickets were drawn and assigned to horses competing in a high profile race, like the English Grand National or the Irish Sweeps Derby. If your horse came first, second, or third, you'd win big bucks, based on the total prize pool.

mechanics of the game. Originally, draws were made using two urns, one filled with pieces of paper bearing player names, the other numbered pieces of paper. It was a laborious process, since the rules dictated that every piece of paper had to be drawn, sometimes taking more than a week to complete. It also encouraged a scam called "bararinaggio," where one person would buy up as many tickets as possible, then resell them at inflated prices. Then, in the 1570s, a clever Genoan hit upon the idea of using numbered balls. The method was first used to select members for the municipal government. Officials placed 120 numbered balls in an urn—one for each candidate—then drew five. It didn't take long for people to start placing little side bets on who would be selected, and soon the little extracurricular activity was more popular than the actual elections. By the middle of the next century, the process was refined—five balls out of 90, a system still used in Italian lotteries today.

By the sixteenth century, a wave of lottomania was sweeping the western world. Italy and France were home to dozens of little draws, while in England, Queen Elizabeth I sponsored a "verie rich Lotterie Generall" with proceeds used to upgrade harbors, support the military and "such other publique goode works." If William Shakespeare bought a ticket, it would have cost him about $2.50 for a one-in-400,000 chance at $25,000 worth of cash and merchandise. Even if he didn't take the jackpot,

Shakespeare would have walked away with something; every ticket collected something for its owner, with a minimum prize equal to about 63 cents. That would pay for a round of ale, with enough left over to put a sizable down-payment on a luxury codpiece.

Over the next two centuries, lotteries became a way of life for Europeans. Everybody got into the act. There were lottery barbers (buy one shave, win a chance on a cash prize!), lottery tailors (buy one pair of pants . . .), even lottery hot dog stands. Riots weren't uncommon, as people stormed ticket offices and fought, literally, to be the first person in line.

Slowly—and rather inexplicably—the public lost interest in lotteries, and by 1826 not only did the British government decide that the glamour was gone from the game, but concluded that lotteries were immoral. There would be one final draw, and that was it. An army of unemployed stormed the streets of London in an advertising blitz: they wore sandwich boards proclaiming, "All Lotteries End Forever! 18th of July!" Even with such marketing savvy, this last lottery did not sell out. It wasn't just the end of an era; in the days before there were any organized revenue-collecting systems, governments had come to rely on lotteries to raise public funds. The death of the lottery marked the birth of modern taxation. Ironically, in another 150 years, the world would return to the lottery to make up for the shortcomings of the system that replaced it.

Meanwhile, the old lottery ways were making their mark on the New World. Some of the earliest lotteries in American were held in Virginia in order to finance its Jamestown colony. The First Great Standing Lottery—a standing lottery is one where all the tickets are sold before the draw can take place—was won by a tailor who took home a hefty 4,000 crowns.

Once the country was up and running, lotteries became a familiar sight. While America had no shortage of goods and trade, there wasn't a lot of cold, hard cash going around. It became common practice for municipal governments to hold lotteries to cover capital expenses like roads, bridges, and civic buildings. Such games of chance enjoyed a relatively solid reputation, and virtually anyone could run a lottery relatively free from government interference.

There are stories of men who held lotteries to get themselves out of debtor's prison, and even such distinguished founding fathers as George Washington, John Hancock, Benjamin Franklin, and Thomas Jefferson liked to test their luck. In fact, in his old age, the bankrupt and destitute Jefferson was granted a special license to run a lottery to raise money for . . . himself.

ONE LUMP OR 25?

A federal law passed shortly before the Lucky 13's big win made it possible for lottery winners to take their jackpot in one lump sum, instead of yearly installments. In one of those rare cases where the government is involved, it actually is a win-win situation.

Although winners get a significantly smaller jackpot than if they went on the installment plan—the lump sum jackpot is roughly equal to the cost of a 20-25 year annuity—a single big payoff is almost always their best option. In this way, debts and taxes can be paid in one go, leaving the winner a lot of money to invest. Since installment payoffs are based on secure investments like government bonds, they don't reflect the rate of return winners could find in a more dynamic portfolio.

Likewise, governments also fare better with lump sum jackpots. Both tax revenue and write-offs increase, since they're not spread over 25 years, which help balance the government books a lot faster.

Soon, it seemed like everyone was getting into the lottery business, but while lots of people claimed to run "national" games, there's been only one true example of this kind in American history. The year was 1776, when the Continental Congress decided that the young country needed some money to carry on its war with England. Taxation was out of the question: that's why they were at war in the first place. Besides, the colonists were strapped for cash. Instead, the government opted for a kind of lottery loan scheme popular with governments of the time. The idea was simple: in exchange for the price of a lottery ticket, players could win up to $50,000 from a $10 million prize pool. In fact, everyone was guaranteed some kind of cash prize. The catch? Prizes over $50 were paid in promissory notes which the winner could redeem after five years. Think of it as an early form of Reaganomics: solving a short-term cash flow crisis by mortgaging the country's future.

There was only one problem with the first, and only, national lottery: nobody bought tickets. Perhaps it was because the prizes just weren't attractive enough to compete with other games of chance, or because Americans, even then, didn't trust their federal government. It could simply have been that nobody had any money. In any case, the draw was delayed, then postponed, then slowly faded away, leaving a few disgruntled ticket-holders and a lot of people left to shake their heads in wonder at the incompetence of their government. For its part, Washington didn't recover from the abysmal failure: the Capital never tried to use lotteries to raise capital again.

The history of lotteries is one of extremes. At one point it seems that no one cares for them, then over time, they become quite the fashion again. In the early part of the 1800s, lotteries were everywhere, but slowly they faded until by the 1860s only three states—Kentucky, Delaware, and Missouri—were running them. The Civil War and its requisite cash flow crunch saw another rise in popularity of the games, and again they seemed as popular as ever. But by 1895 they were banned from coast to coast. What happened? It seems that one by one, the state lotteries were overwhelmed by mismanagement and corruption until there was only one left.

The Louisiana State Lottery Company began at the end of the Civil War and granted absolute control over all gambling and gaming in the state. Exempt from all taxes, the company had a 25-year deal for an annual fee of $40,000. Although headed by two former Confederate generals, the company itself was actually a front for a group of rather shady New York backers, who'd use their success to influence an entire generation of Louisiana politicians. Within ten years, the Louisiana lottery company had evolved into a powerful political machine with several hundred million dollars in assets. In fact, it was too big for some people, and in 1871 the state legislature tried to crush the company and its northern masters. However, at the constitutional convention, lottery officials bought up as many delegates as it could. Not only was the lottery's charter upheld at the conference, the company's powers were increased. It now had the power to license other lottery companies for a $40,000 fee. Lottery officials had learned the power of advertising and, since they held a virtual monopoly on lotteries in the country, targeted people living in America's richest states. The lottery sold 90 percent of its tickets outside of Louisiana; 30 percent of all mail passing through the state was directly related to the lottery. The company reaped profits of more than $12 million a year—talk about your Louisiana purchase—and while much of it went to support state social services like education and health, the lion's share went to bribes, directors' fees, and shareholders.

By the end of the 25-year charter, most people in Louisiana, if not the country, had had enough of the lottery company. It had become a symbol of the greed and corruption that many felt was sinking the American political system. Louisiana's governor fought against any renewal of the charter, but the company was far too powerful to give up without a fight.

CANADIAN LOTTO HISTORY IN A NUTSHELL

 **1968.** In May, Montreal Mayor Jean Drapeau introduces his "voluntary tax": for two dollars, taxpayers get a chance at $150,000 in silver ingots. The idea lasts for several draws before the federal government puts an end to it.

1969. The federal government changes the criminal code to allow provinces to operate and license lottery schemes; most other games of chance, however, are still illegal.

1970. Ready, willing, and able, the province of Quebec takes the lead in the lottery race. Their first venture is called Inter Plus; it's an offshoot of Drapeau's "tax," with a two-dollar ticket giving you a chance at a $150,000 grand prize. The inaugural draw is held March 14. Manitoba also launches its own Manitoba Centennial Sweepstakes, with proceeds earmarked for that province's 100th birthday celebration.

1973. The Federal Olympic Act authorizes Quebec to run a national lottery to raise money for the 1976 Olympics. In the nine draws between 1973 and 1976, the Olympic Lottery raises $255 million, proving that lotteries were as big a cash cow as the Big O itself would prove to be a white elephant.

1974. British Columbia, Alberta, Saskatchewan, and Manitoba form the Western Canada Lottery Corporation—proving once again that politics makes strange, and uncomfortable, bedfellows.

1975. Ontario jumps into the lottery fire in February, and launches its biweekly Wintario draw.

1976. The Feds launch Loto Canada, a national draw with proceeds earmarked for the ever-expanding Olympic debt. The provinces protest, claiming that the feds are now breaking their own laws; in August, Ontario and the four western provinces join forces in the Interprovincial Lottery Corporation (ILC). The four Atlantic provinces

It battled through every step in the legislature, finally forcing the governor to put the matter to public vote. But before the people had their say, the Postmaster General of the United States had his say. He banished all lottery material from the federal mail system, a move supported by Congress which in turn banned all lottery ticket sales and promotions. At first, the Louisiana State Lottery Company tried to buck the system by setting up shop offshore in Honduras, but Congress countered with an also start their own lottery company.

1977. Lotteries now play coast to coast: Canadians spend $25 per capita on lottery tickets this year.

1978. Ottawa announces Loto Select, a $1 game based on Loto-Quebec's 6/36 game. Ontario and Quebec respond with plans for a computerized lottery. But in August, the Trudeau government offers a compromise: the feds will run only $10-plus lottos, if the provinces stick to $9-or-less ones.

1979. Joe Clark's newly elected Conservative government politely bows out of the lottery game, thanks to some gentle diplomacy, and a $24 million-per-year golden handshake from the provinces.

1980. The ILC starts Super Lotto, a $10 game to fill the Loto Canada void.

1982. In June, the ILC introduces its game superstar, Lotto 6/49, offering big prizes and hideous odds.

1984. The feds dive back in to the pool . . .the baseball pool, that is. In March, they launch Sports Select Baseball, but it strikes out, losing millions of dollars in a matter of months. By the year's end, the feds promise to stay out of the lottery game, no fooling this time. As a token of the provinces' good faith, the feds ask for an additional $100 million to help pay for the huge debt incurred by the Calgary Winter Olympics . . .is there a pattern developing here?

1985. In April, British Columbia takes its bouncy balls, goes home, and starts its own lottery company. The province quickly becomes national leader in embarrassing lottery scandals.

1989. The Crystal Casino—complete with its absurd dress code—opens its doors in Winnipeg. It's the first permanent casino in the country, although others will soon follow.

1990. Video lottery terminals are introduced in Atlantic Canada, thus signaling the end of civilization as we know it.

---

out and out ban on imported or interstate lottery trade. The year was 1895; the country would not see another legal lottery for 70 years.

The key word is legal. For the first 60 years of the 20th century, lotteries went underground. While some people ventured south to play Mexico's national lottery—which had been around in one form or another since the 1770s—the heart of the lotto black market was located north of the border, in the Canadian province of Quebec, where the

Catholic sensibility was more open to this sort of fundraising. Eric Bender, in his 1938 book *Tickets to Fortune*, fingered Canada as a source of most of the illegal lottery scams inundating the U.S. "Quebec and Montreal are the key cities in the racket," Bender complains. "The Premier of the Province of Quebec gets countless letters every year asking for information about specific schemes. To all such requests he can only answer that all lotteries are illegal, and therefore he cannot officially recognize the existence of any of them."

Throughout the 1940s and 1950s, public opinion shifted in favor of lotteries. Again, much of the pressure for reinstating lotteries in North America came from Canada, where a 1953 poll showed 85 percent of the population supported the idea of lotteries aimed to raise money for health and welfare programs. Politicians started to speak out in favor of lotteries—led by Quebec's Premier Maurice Duplessis—and pointed to overseas successes like the Irish Sweepstakes and, most of all, England's soccer pools. Every Commonwealth country except Canada ran such pools, in which players would bet a small amount on the outcome of several soccer games. The payout was very good—a two-cent bet could net $300,000 for a winner—and by the early 1960s a quarter of a million Canadians were regularly playing the British pools. At the height of their popularity, football pools were the sixth largest industry in England, and prompted the Football Association to complain that 16 times as many played the pools as watched the sport.

Meanwhile, the citizens of Montreal continued to take their chances on illegal, home-grown lotteries. *Maclean's* magazine reported that in 1963, lotteries were a $25-million-a-year business in that city. The magazine went on to quote a Montreal judge who lamented, as he passed sentence on a lottery operator, that it did not seem "wholly consistent to send a modern lottery operator to the institution which is the descendant of the lottery-built Montreal jail of the eighteenth century." Meanwhile, numbers runners in states like New Jersey and New York were doing a booming business. Perhaps it was the success of these illegal lotteries that prompted New Hampshire to take a chance on games of chance. In 1964 the state started its Sweepstakes, with profits earmarked to boost New Hampshire's education system. For three bucks, players took a chance on the results of a horse race. It was a complicated affair, with a low return; unlike today's lotto games, which regularly contribute 40-60 percent of sales to the prize pool, the New Hampshire Sweepstakes ponied up a measly one percent of sales. It was a calculated bet; the state believed that the public was more open to the idea of a lottery than a tax hike. And while ticket sales were fairly sluggish at first, the government had accurately read the mood of the people. There was little public outcry to the lottery; the die was cast.

Three years later, New York started its own lottery. Again, sales were sluggish, but not because people were opposed to it. Typically, the government misread the mood of the people: they didn't mind the lottery, but what they really wanted was better games with more attractive odds and bigger prizes. By the mid-1970s, ten states were holding lotteries and total sales were approaching the billion-dollar-a-year mark. Then came the 1980s, and suddenly things changed. In the first year of the decade, lotto sales totaled just over $2 billion; ten years later, 37 states and the District of Columbia were in the lottery business, racking up total sales of $20 billion a year. What happened? Once again, simple math was a factor. More states means more players means more sales. But that doesn't account for the growth in popularity. New Hampshire offers a good example. In the first ten or so years of operation, the state lottery grew about 70 percent; not bad for a state that experienced only modest population growth during the same time period. However, from the mid-1970s to 1990 lotto sales in New Hampshire increase 950 percent.

What was the secret?

Advances in computer technology surely made a difference. By the early 1980s, most lottery companies offered at least one online game, which made for a faster, more efficient system, and making it possible for organizers to offer large-scale, multi-state games. But just as important, the lottery companies were becoming more savvy. They realized that people weren't buying lotto tickets because it looked good on the resume. Players wanted big games with big jackpots. In the early seventies, a million-dollar ticket was front page news. But by the mid-1980s, players wanted one thing: record-breaking jackpots. Which brings us back to 1984, a pivotal year in lottery history. That's when lotteries really caught on in America, and it seemed that a jackpot record would be set only to give way to a new one a few weeks later. In May, four New Yorkers held tickets on a $22 million payday. Barely one month later, Americans were lining up for hours to get a chance on the Massachusetts' Megabucks $15.6 million grand prize. Only one person held the lucky ticket, earning himself a place in the record books for the largest unshared lotto win.

But the record was short-lived. A few weeks later, on July 26, New York's Venero Pagano won $20 million in that state's lottery, the biggest prize ever awarded to a single ticket holder. Pagano, a retired carpenter, seemed overwhelmed by his win, and had no idea what to do with all that money. "I got whatever I need," he told reporters at the press conference. "I got my tomatoes; I will continue to grow tomatoes in my yard." As

WHAT'S YOUR L.Q.?

Lots of people, are big fans of the lottery, and can't imagine a week without their lottery "fix." Take this simple test to determine your L.Q.—your Lottery Quotient.

Directions:
1. Using a sharp pencil, circle the correct response.
2. Check your score at the end of this test.
3. Remember at all times to keep tongue firmly in cheek.

1. Finish this sentence. "I buy lottery tickets . . ."
   a) Once a month.
   b) Once a week.
   c) More than once a week.
   d) Sorry, I don't have time to finish the sentence. I have to go buy another lottery ticket.

2. "6/49" is:
   a) A complicated sexual position.
   b) Your odds on winning the lottery.
   c) .12224489.
   d) None of the above.

3. "Scratch and win" is:
   a) An "active" lottery game.
   b) A strategy used by most major league baseball players.

4. I think that some of the Multi-State Lottery Association money should be set aside to:
   a) Pay for social services and medical research.
   b) Buy William Shatner a really good hair piece.

5. The first American lottery of the modern era was a sweepstakes-style lottery, involving horses and a numbered draw. Why did organizers abandon these kinds of sweepstakes?
   a) They were too complicated for the average player to follow.
   b) They couldn't get the horses to stay in that little drum.

6. The odds of winning Powerball are 80 million to 1. You have a better chance of:
   a) Being struck buy lightning.
   b) Being groped by Bill Clinton.

7. Complete this sentence. "Sales of lottery tickets should be restricted to . . .":
   a) Persons over the age of eighteen.
   b) Me.

8. Have you ever tried the "quick pick"?
   a) Yes, all the time.
   b) Yes, but only when I'm in a hurry.
   c) Yes, but only when I'm sure no one is watching.

9. Experts now consider lotteries highly addictive to:
   a) The people who play them.
   b) The governments who run them.

10. Complete this sentence. "I think that the government should provide professional counseling for . . .":
    a) People who win jackpots in excess of $1 million.
    b) People who come up with those annoying lottery ads.

Score

Give yourself five points for every right answer. Subtract ten points if you took this test seriously. Add 20 points if you had to stop half-way through to double-check your lottery ticket numbers.

Rating

0 - 10 points: *Lotto-Illiterate*. You have about as much chance of becoming a lottery addict as you have of winning the next Powerball draw.

15 - 30 points: *Lotto-Lout*. Maybe soon you'll get around to checking your Big Game numbers.

35 - 50 points: *Lotto Lover*. Bet you have calluses on your scratching finger.

50+ points: *Lotto-Loonie*. It's official, you're a lottery loonie. There's no hope for you—unless of course, you win the big one.

summer rolled in, luck American-style was in full swing, as folks scrambled to buy tickets—at a rate of 14,000 per minute—on the Illinois lottery's $40 million prize.

By the end of 1984, lottomania was in full swing. Gross sales neared the $10 billion mark in America alone, and over the next five years that total doubled again. In fact, in 1990, *Forbes* magazine ranked state-run lotteries 24th in gross sales among American companies—tying with communications giant ITT. Collectively, U.S. lotteries saw a net profit of $10 billion that year, on sales of $20 billion. Compare that to IBM, who turned a $6 billion profit on $70 billion sales, and you understand why lotteries have become big business for big governments. Meanwhile, around the world, the lottery craze was in full swing. By 1990, 110 countries held lotteries of one kind or another; in North America alone, 32 states, the District of Columbia, nine Canadian provinces, and Mexico were all in the lottery business. By now, lotteries weren't just seen as a necessary evil, a voluntary tax aimed to cover the costs of ever-increasing social services, but as a legitimate, acceptable form of entertainment.

Across the pond, lottery fever was established in 1930 with the Irish Sweepstakes, with profits going to hospitals. How successful was the Sweeps? In its first ten years, it brought in more than $2.5 billion; that's a lot of bedpans and bandages. Everybody played the game, despite it being illegal, to the point that the New York City trial of two Sweeps ticket sellers was delayed for two weeks while the court searched for twelve honest jurors . . . who'd never bought a ticket.

By the 1960s, *Saturday Night* estimated that Canadians alone spent $25 million annually on the Sweeps. The magazine went on to say that the 20-foot-long, nine-foot-deep Sweepstakes draw drum in Dublin "has become one of Europe's great tourist attractions," and that the lottery company itself was the second largest employer in Ireland.

Perhaps the most famous Sweepstakes story of all concerned an unemployed machinist from Oakland, California named Frank McNulty. In 1973, he won $128,000. He dumped most of his winnings into a bank in Jersey, a British tax haven. When the Internal Revenue Service came calling for its share, the fiery Irish-American told them to take a hike, or words to that effect. He was arrested and, on St. Patrick's Day, 1975, sentenced to five years of hard time. He served most of the sentence, never yielding to the taxman's demands, and in the process became a folk hero.

By the late 1970s the Sweeps was being swept up by the competition. Most countries had their own legal lotteries, offering simpler rules and bigger payouts, and by 1980 the Irish Hospital Sweepstakes drew its final breath. The Luck of the Irish had succumbed to the Luck Of The Draw.

TOP 20 LOTTERY JACKPOTS

1. Illinois/Michigan	$363.0 million	2*	May 9, 2000 The Big Game
2. Indiana	$295.7 million	1	July 29, 1998 Powerball
3. Massachusetts	$197 million	1	April 6, 1999 The Big Game
4. Wisconsin	$194.5 million	1	May 20, 1998 Powerball
5. Minnesota	$151 million	1	June 30, 1999 Powerball
6. Minnesota/Kansas/ Missouri	$150.2 million	3	March 4 2000 Powerball
7. California	$118.8 million	10	April 17, 1991
8. Georgia	$116 million	1	Aug. 3, 1999 The Big Game
9. Pennsylvania	$115.6 million	14	April 26, 1989
10. Wisconsin	$111.2 million	1	July 7, 1993 Powerball
11. Florida	$106.5 million	6	Sept. 15, 1990
12. California	$104 million	3	April 8, 1998
13. Arizona	$101.8 million	1	March 4, 1995 Powerball
14. Indianna/ Nebraska	$101 million	2	Nov. 30, 1994 Powerball
15. New York	$100 million	1	Dec. 31, 1999
16. New York	$90 million	9	Jan. 26, 1991
17. Florida	$89.8 million	6	Oct. 26, 1991
18. D.C.	$89.5 million	2	Dec. 22, 1993
19. Kentucky	$89.3 million	1	Jan. 24, 1996
20. Idaho	$87.6 million	1	June 3, 1995

*=number of winning tickets

Chapter 3

Players

Has the growth of lotteries slowed since 1990? Don't bet on it. Total sales of lottery tickets and other state-run gambling monopolies have doubled again, and now exceed $40 billion in the U.S. alone.

Who buys lottery tickets? The quick answer is, who doesn't? Between 60 to 75 percent of Americans buy lottery tickets at least occasionally, while more than 40 percent play lotto on a regular basis. How regularly? A survey in the January 1998 issue of *Demographics* claims that 42 percent of men and 34 percent of women play the lottery at least once a week. And forget those old wive's tales of lottery players being poverty-stricken gambling junkies. Surveys show that the average ticket buyer is a middle-income earner who rarely gambles outside of the lottery; someone just like you, particularly if you are male: men are 20 percent more likely to play the lottery than women.

Persistence is the hallmark of the lottery player. Most of the winners and players we spoke to had been buying tickets for at least ten years, and planned to keep buying until the end of time. Oregon's Michael Schulte is a typical die-hard player. Every Tuesday and Thursday, this 62-year-old retired machinist buys Powerball tickets. Schulte, who's worked hard all his life and still holds down a part-time job as a security guard, says that it's a ritual he's been keeping up for almost ten years.

"Every time I buy a lottery ticket I'm certain it's a winner," Schulte told me. "But if it isn't a winner it doesn't mean I'm going to quit. I don't give up that easily."

LEGAL EAGLES

The September 1994 issue of *Harper's* magazine reported that a woman sued the Pennsylvania lottery commission for $1.5 million. The reason? Seems she was upset because, despite all the money she'd spent, she'd never won the state lottery.

Like a lot of players, Schulte says that there's a simple reason he plays the lottery: he wants to win The Big One.

"I'm not greedy; I'd be happy with just a million dollars, " Schulte says. "That's enough to pay off the rest of our mortgage, help our kids out a little, and let us do some travelling. It would be nice not to worry about bills for once in our life."

When it comes to the all-important question—why play lotteries?— Schulte isn't too sure of the answer. Like most people, he doesn't really think a lottery windfall will change his life. In fact, in a survey published in *Adweek Magazine*, more than 60 percent of respondents said that they didn't think winning the lottery would make them happier. Meanwhile, even more people said that even if they won $10 million, they wouldn't quit working.

"I'm not so sure about that," says Schulte. "If I won the lottery I'd kiss off my part-time job in a second. I'd much rather be lying on a beach somewhere, sunning myself, or out in the boat, fishing."

Schulte does admit that one of the reasons he started playing the lottery was his lack of any real savings plan. Again, this puts him in good company. Most Americans subscribe to the erroneous belief that it's easier to get rich by winning a lottery than by saving and investing over time. Even the odds don't deter him. Despite the fact that lotteries offer by far the worst odds of any form of gambling—lotteries pay back 14 cents on of every dollar spent, while the average casino game pays back 90 cents or more—and nowhere near the return of even a moderately risky stock, people like Schulte prefer investing in the luck of the draw.

"I never was that great at saving money. My wife and I tried and we do have a little socked away, but not nearly enough to live off of the rest of our lives. Of course, my wife and I both have small pensions, and they help. But when you get right down to it, we could sure use a big, juicy jackpot."

When it comes to playing the lottery, Schulte chooses to ignore the simple truth: math is against you. Earl Rosenbloom is an Associate

LOOKING FOR THAT LUCKY BREAK

Some people will go to any length to play their favorite lottery game. One day Donald Snow, of New Brunswick, Canada, decided to take a break and go buy a lottery ticket. . . .

A prison break, that is.

In the spring of 1994, Snow walked away from the Westmorland Institute, a minimum security prison near Moncton. He strolled down to the nearest corner store, several miles away, and bought a ticket on that night's Loto 6/49 draw.

Guards finally caught him, trying to break back into the prison.

"My intention was to win $10 million," Snow explained to the judge. He didn't. But he did get a bonus: the judge added 15 days to his sentence.

Snow's story doesn't quite top Michel Laurier's, who won half a million dollars on the Olympic Lottery in the summer of 1976. The catch was, he'd stolen his ticket by holding up, at gun point, a Montreal branch of the Royal Bank. He fled with $3,856 cash, plus 40 lottery tickets that the bank was planning to sell, one of which proved to be a winner. It was the perfect crime until—you guessed it—Laurier tried to collect on his winning ticket!

Thanks to his good luck, Laurier wound up with 13 years in the slammer. And what happened to the prize money? It was awarded to the Royal Bank, who donated the money to Canada's Olympic training program.

Professor in the Faculty of Management at the University of Manitoba, specializing in mathematical models for business. As a passing fancy, he's also turned his fondness for figures to games of chance, like horse racing, lotteries, and blackjack. Rosenbloom says that lottery players, in the long run, are guaranteed one thing.

"If you play long enough, you will lose money. If you're looking for a good investment, then the lottery isn't it. However, if you're looking for some entertainment, and you enjoy playing the lottery, then that's a different story."

Rosenbloom says that he has no moral objection to the lottery or other forms of gambling—he's particularly fond of the ponies himself—

BETTER BETTING

 Ben E. Johnson is the author of three books on lotteries, including *Winning the Lottery* and, most recently, *Getting Lucky*. He also writes "The Lottery Column," which is syndicated throughout the U.S. He says that there is no secret formula for snagging a lotto jackpot, but there are some strategies you can use to improve your chances. Ben suggests:

1. Join a lottery pool. "If you can afford $5 a week, that gives you five chances a week to win; if you have 20 friends who can afford $5 a week, that gives you one hundred chances a week."

2. Play your favorite game only once a week. "If you have two draws on a lotto game in a week, don't play both of them. Put all your money on one draw and that doubles your chances right there."

3. Be aware of the odds. "Not every lottery game has the same odds. It's surprising how many people don't understand this. People should look around and find the best odds for their money."

4. Ask for lottery tickets for gifts. "There are many, many people who've won very large amounts of money by getting lottery tickets as presents."

5. Use the quick pick rather than your own "lucky" numbers. "Don't pick lucky numbers; they just aren't that lucky. There's no special that they have over random selection, and chances are random selection has fewer people who have the same numbers as when you play them. The fewer people who share your numbers, the fewer people you have to share your jackpot with if you win."

6. Avoid "hot" and "cold" numbers. "The whole foundation of the lottery is that you cannot predict any kind of winning pattern, or winning numbers. Over time, all numbers win at about the same frequency."

7. Avoid popular numbers. "If you're going to win, you're better off winning with numbers nobody else has."

8. Avoid scams and systems. "There is no one set of winning numbers that has ever been picked more than once, in all the lotteries across the United States and Canada. Lottery numbers truly are randomly selected. . . . In other words, if anyone offers to sell you a system that will beat the lotteries, don't believe it."

PLAYING THE LOTTERY IS GOOD FOR YOUR HEALTH

The news wasn't good for John Evanco.

In the summer of 1982, doctors told this resident of Waukesha, Wisconsin that he had throat cancer. One of the first things he did was give up smoking, and he decided to use the money he saved on cigarettes to buy lottery tickets.

Six years later, and two years after the last signs of his cancer had disappeared, John's healthy lifestyle paid an unexpected dividend. On Christmas Eve, 1987, John, his wife, and their two daughters split a $39.5 million jackpot in the Illinois State lottery. John proves, once and for all, that playing the lottery is good for your health.

but thinks it's helpful if people go into these games of chance with a realistic understanding of what they're dealing with. At times, even the terms we use to talk about the lottery can be deceptive.

"You can't really talk about 'odds'; that refers to a one-time bet, and reflects the bettor's perception of a possible outcome. As far as lotteries are concerned, you're dealing with chance in probability."

In other words, while your chances of picking the winning set of six numbers in the next Lotto 6/49 is somewhere in the neighborhood of one in 14 million, no bookie on earth is going to offer odds on you being the jackpot winner. There's not even a guarantee that anybody will win the jackpot. Having said all that, Rosenbloom reluctantly offers this advice to lottery aficionados: wait until the jackpot increases.

"It won't improve your chance of winning, but it means that the payoff is higher if your bet comes through. Of course, generally, as the jackpot starts to get bigger, more people play, so there's a greater chance you'll have to share your prize."

For his part, Michael Schulte has vowed to keep buying lottery tickets until his lotto dream comes true. And while persistence is the hallmark of players like Schulte, when it comes to lotteries, it is possible to try too hard. Just ask the people of Assiniboia, a Canadian farming community in the province of Saskatchewan. In the spring of 1981, Joseph Tremblay walked into the Western Canada Lottery office in Winnipeg to claim a million dollar jackpot. But something about the ticket didn't jibe for lottery officials, so they delayed Tremblay's payment while the backroom boys ran some tests.

SYSTEMS CHECK

Everybody's got one. And whether you're aware of it or not, you've got one, too. A system, that is; a strategy you use to, hopefully, increase your chance of winning the big draw.

Maybe it's nothing more than superstition—you only buy tickets on odd-numbered days, for example—or maybe you spend hours poring over lists of past lotto winners, searching for the next winning combination. No matter what, if you play with any regularity, you've got a system.

Systems are personal things: formulas for success that we only share with our closest friends and loved ones. But that's not the case for Al Klestil. This electrical technician and computer programmer from Victoria, B.C. has a system which he says is guaranteed to improve your chance of winning a lottery. And he's willing to share his secret for next to nothing; all you need is a computer and a telephone.

Klestil is President of LottoWare, a Canadian company that manufactures and markets lottery software packages. It's a good starting point for anyone interested in lottery systems because it combines "wheeling" and "historic analysis," the two most popular strategies used by serious lottery players.

"You have to realize what the lotto program is for," Klestil says. "It's not for you to get rich or for you to get the jackpot on the first try, that's not what the program is good for. What it can do is help you analyze past lotteries, and organize your number selections to cover the most ground."

Klestil doesn't make any grandiose claims about his computer program,

The suspicions were confirmed. Tremblay's winner was actually two tickets spliced together: four digits from one ticket—on its own, good for $1,000—and two digits from another.

Within minutes, the police arrived to question Tremblay, who admitted the ticket was a fake. He was desperate for cash, he explained, to cover a $225,000 stock market loss. And that wasn't all. Turns out this small-time crook was also His Honor, the Mayor of Assiniboia. The mayor faced numerous fraud charges that could have landed him up to 14 years in prison.

In court, Tremblay's lawyer explained that he had sold his farm equip-

and cautions against any system that promises to unlock the secrets of the lottery.

"You don't start using a system because you want to win the jackpot. If someone tells you to buy their lotto system because you will win a big jackpot, that's just not true. A true system helps you target small prizes, to improve your chances of winning your investment back."

Klestil grew up around legal lotteries. He's a native of Czechoslovakia—the former name of the independent Czech and Slovak republics—where they've been playing lotteries for hundreds of years. As a teenager, Klestil's father started him playing the Czech equivalent of Lotto 6/49 and taught him "wheeling," the betting strategy at the heart of many computer lottery programs.

"The only sure way of winning a lottery is to cover every possible number combinations, but who can do that? Wheeling is a way of targeting fewer numbers by covering all possible combinations of a small range of numbers."

Historical analysis is another popular system used by serious lottery players. It involves a careful review of numbers drawn on a particular game. Players look for "hot" and "cold" numbers—those drawn more or less frequently than others—and "twin" or friendly numbers, ones that tend to be drawn together. There are also enemy numbers which, you guessed it, rarely get picked in the same draw.

Finally, serious numeroholics want to know which numbers are most popular . . .so that they can avoid them. In most lotteries, people play 7, 11, and 3 more than any other numbers; if you play them and win the jackpot, there's a greater chance you'll have to share.

ment business in 1979, but had lost it all buying oil futures on the stock market. "His whole life's efforts are gone and in a desperate attempt to recoup his losses, he began buying lottery tickets by the handful," Tremblay's lawyer told the judge. In the end, the judge gave Tremblay a six-month conditional discharge, and ordered him to donate the amount of his legitimate lottery win, $1,000, to charity.

Like Joseph Tremblay, Patricia Smith let the lure of the lottery get the better of her, and what started off as an innocent pastime soon deteriorated into a criminal addiction. Maybe things would have turned out differently if Smith had held another job; as a teller in an Ontario trust company, she had access to the endless stream of cash that powered her compulsion. She developed a simple, bold system: she'd skim off a few bills whenever she transferred cash from the vault to her drawer. Later, she wrote bogus checks on the company's internal account to cover her tracks. Soon, Smith was taking home a $5,000 bonus every week, all of which went into Lottario tickets.

When the police finally caught up with her, Smith had run up over half a million dollars in false transactions, although the trust company pegged its real losses at just over $180,000. She'd also won $27,000 on the lottery, but most of that money went back in to feeding her habit.

"This is actually a sad case," Smith's lawyer told Canadian Press. "You can see the logic of it to her—if she's the biggest player of Lottario she's sooner or later going to be the big winner."

One of the most ambitious attempts was made by Tom and Philomena Drake, a couple from McMurray, Pennsylvania who became American folk heroes in the late 1970s as they sunk their life savings into the state lottery. "We're selling everything except our clothes and our furniture and enough to pay the rent," Tom Drake told reporters. "When we win the million, we'll do what we want for the rest of our lives." Tom, a real estate agent, took his inspiration from the lead character in the Sylvester Stallone movie *Rocky*. "Nobody thought he had a chance," Drake said of the fictional boxer. "But he believed in himself and he did it. So why couldn't I?"

Frustrated with the daily grind, which yielded a combined salary of $20,000, the Drakes decided to quit their jobs and play the lottery full-time. For seven hours every day, they sat at a special table in the McMurray Pharmacy, where they scratched their daily quota of 200 tickets. They were playing a bingo-style game, where certain combinations of numbers in a row awarded either a cash prize up to $10,000, or the chance at a bonus draw where the grand prize was $1,000 a week for life. The Drakes' goal was to buy 20,000 of the $1 tickets, but they ran out of time and money at around 14,000. That still sounds like a lot, but with 35 million tickets in circulation, the Drakes' chances were remote.

There is a happy ending to this story. No, the underdog Drakes didn't throw a last minute, knock-out punch. But they did earn a split decision. While they didn't get a shot at the $1 million bonus draw, they did win $1,000 more than they spent on tickets.

Canada's answer to the Drakes was an Ontario electronics technician named Suky Bacvic. In the winter of 1978, Bacvic sold his house in Hamilton for a cool $50,000 profit. At first, he thought he'd buy another house with the money. But then he saw a lottery ad on TV: "Picture yourself a millionaire," the ad urged. That was it for Bacvic; he bought $10 lottery tickets throughout southern Ontario.

"Once I decided, there were no half measures," Bacvic told the *Toronto Star*. "I sank the whole lot in to Loto Canada tickets. With so many tickets, I figured I had to win."

The ticket draw was held early in December. Six months later, Bacvic finished checking the last of his 5,000 tickets. For all his efforts, he'd won a grand total of $1,300. As a small consolation, though, he did pick up a bonus prize of a trip for two to anywhere in Canada. He sent in his winning ticket, and a few days later he got a call that his travel vouchers were ready. He picked up his prize, only to discover that the vouchers expired that very day. He asked the lottery company and the airline to extend the deadline, but they wouldn't budge. By the end of his experience, Bacvic—who'd never gambled before—was bitter and angry, and swore never to buy lottery tickets again.

"You know, these tickets look like money, but they're just garbage," he complained. "I think the Loto Canada hooks the people with lots of small cash prizes, but how many people get close to the big money?"

CHAPTER 4

WINNERS

It's one thing to dream about winning the lottery, and another thing entirely when that dream comes true. Just ask John and Sandy Jarrell. According to a profile in the April 1999 issue of *Money*, the Jarells weren't quite prepared for the media frenzy that followed their win. When they got home from work that day, they found a hoard of reporters and television cameras outside their house. John gave a short interview, and hoped that was the end of that. But a steady stream of reporters continued to call and drop by for weeks.

All the attention took its toll, and when the local newspaper published their address, the Jarrells got nervous. John took to keeping a loaded pistol by the bed. Within weeks they bought a home in the country; it was as much an escape as a move up. Over time, the family adjusted to their new-found financial security, but discovered that while the money hadn't changed them, it sure changed the attitude of some of the people around them: both he and his wife found that some of their old friends had abandoned them. In the meantime, John continued to work at his old job, although he was able to cut his hours in half. It's a story echoed time and time again by lottery winners.

Roy Kaplan, a sociologist who lives in Tampa Bay, Florida, spent 20 years studying the behavior of North America's lottery winners. He says that while a lottery win may make you richer, it won't change your lifestyle overnight. "Most winners will tell you that their lives haven't changed; they're doing the same things they always did, just more of it."

In 1978, Kaplan was teaching at a university in Buffalo, with a keen interest in the meaning of work to people, when he published *Lottery Winners: How They Won And How Winning Changed Their Lives.* The book was the result of seven years of interviews with American lottery winners. Kaplan says that, despite claims that their lives haven't changed, most winners found that their relationships with friends and family members were often strained by their windfall.

"No one is prepared for the public exposure that can follow a big lottery win," Kaplan says. "Many winners get a flood of mail, everything from well-wishers and marriage proposals, to threats and people asking for money. Even winners who don't directly experience problems live in a state of anxiety. They've heard the stories and know that the potential for problems is always out there."

Perhaps the biggest thing lottery winners have to deal with is the sense of isolation. While Powerball's Lucky 13 have faired better than others—most of them still work together and can lean on each other—the average winner has few people to turn to for support.

"Often, they live in a kind of self-imposed isolation. There's a genuine sense of fear, but there's also a sense that friends and family members can no longer be completely trusted. Winners often suspect their friend's motives, and notice that some people's attitudes have changed in subtle ways."

Today Kaplan is Executive Director of the Tampa Bay chapter of the National Council of Christians and Jews, but he still does consulting work for various lotteries. He says that, despite what winners will tell you, he doesn't think anyone can remain the same after experiencing the luck of the draw.

"Some people would admit that it had been traumatic, in that their lives have been fundamentally altered. I think essentially everybody was far more secure economically than before they won; as one guy told me, he felt like a thousand pounds was lifted from his shoulders. All things considered, we should be so lucky to have their problems."

The odds of winning the jackpot on Canada's old Super Loto game were 800,000 to one. The odds of winning it twice were 1,075,308,603 to one; in other words, virtually nil. One was just as likely to be hit by a falling meteor, get eaten by a shark, or get struck by lightning. But Pierre Casault did just that: on July 13, 1982, he won $1 million on Super Loto. Less than

I Won! Now What?

It's ten o'clock on Saturday night and a voice on the radio tells you that you've just won The Big One. Before you pop that cork, sign the back of your ticket. You might want to make a photocopy of the ticket as well, just in case.

Now comes the hard part: where to hide the thing. Some sleep with it under their pillows or stick it under the mattress—one excited Vancouver woman even hid her winning ticket in a block of cheese overnight. Gemma Cote of Quebec City had a cool idea: after winning $5 million, she hid the ticket in her freezer. Talk about cold cash. . . .

three years later, on February 4, 1983, he collected a second million dollar prize.

"It's fantastic, it's unbelievable," he told the press at the time.

Pierre seemed a model winner. He made himself readily available for interviews and radio phone-in shows. And he took great pains to look after his money. He hired $100-an-hour advisers to help him manage his money, and by the end of 1983 had built up a $2.5 million portfolio in stocks and real estate. But the pressure was building. After his first win, he stayed on with his job as auditor at the Royal Bank, but after his second jackpot, he was so pestered for tips from co-workers that he quit. With time on his hands, he threw himself into various projects—a fire safety board game, a line of Amway-style products for Quebecers—and eventually bought a restaurant, where he kept himself so busy that his wife complained she saw him less than ever. In November, 1986, Pierre told a reporter for Southam News that he'd grown depressed and had to see a therapist to help him adjust to his bout with luck.

"This is not an easy thing to deal with, suddenly becoming wealthy," Pierre said. "It was tough on me and it was tough on my relationship with my wife."

Believe it or not, Pierre is not the only person to win two major lottery prizes. It happens more often than you'd think; the list includes an unidentified woman in the late 1980s who won the New York State lottery twice in four months, collecting untold millions, and defying odds of 17 trillion to one.

BRITS HIT THE BIG TIME

 Although people in Britain have been enjoying sports pools for years, lotteries are a fairly recent phenomenon. In November 1999, British lottery organizers celebrated their fifth anniversary by releasing the results of a winners' survey. Organizers questioned 250 people who'd won prizes ranging from $100,000 to several million dollars. The results:

- 55 percent said they were happier now than before their win.
- Only 2 percent said they were less happy.
- 95 percent of the married winners remained together after the win.
- 83 percent of winners had given some money to family members.
- Men surveyed were more generous with their winnings; on average, men gave away more money to a wider range of friends than women.
- 60 percent of the winners had not moved.
- Half the winners were still working; however, only 27 percent of winning $4 million or more were still working.
- 1 percent of winners had plastic surgery.
- 90 percent of winners still played the lottery.

Like other retired people, David Currie (not his real name) had certain informal rituals he liked to perform. Every Monday morning, for example, he'd sit down with a copy of *The Toronto Star* and check his numbers on Saturday's Lotto 6/49 draw. Canada's most popular national lottery is a simple enough game to play: you pick six numbers from 1 to 49 (hence the name), and hope they match the six numbers drawn. No problem at all, if you don't take into account that the odds of winning are one in 13,983,816. Dave's wife Elizabeth got him started on the game. She'd spend up to $40 a week, dreaming of the day when luck would be on her side and she'd win the big jackpot. After Liz passed away in 1993, Dave still played, just for the fun of it.

On Monday, January 3, 1994, David picked up the paper and turned to the lottery page. He scanned his picks for that New Year's Day draw. Nothing. Then he checked his Celebration '94 ticket. Unlike Lotto 6/49, Celebration had preprinted numbers and came in a sealed envelope; it's

MY KINGDOM FOR A KIDNEY

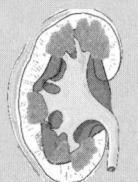 British lotto winner Nick Taylor came up with a novel way to spend his $6.5 million jackpot: he bought himself a new organ.

No, it wasn't a Wurlitzer or Hammond; it was a kidney. Taylor, who'd been suffering kidney disease since he was 11, offered to exchange his windfall for a healthy organ. His idea drew criticism from doctors in Britain, where it's illegal to pay for a transplanted organ—but caught the attention of dozens of willing donors.

In the end, Taylor, who'd endured two failed transplants and ongoing dialysis treatment, was told he'd have to wait his turn for a transplant like everyone else.

one of the ILC's "Special Events" draws, occasional lotteries which feature a number of big prizes, and which are hailed as one of the best bets of any lottery in the world. This 1994 edition featured a $5 million grand prize and five $1 million second-place prizes. Dave spotted his number right away among the million dollar winners.

"The only regret I have is that my wife wasn't here to share it. She would have gone nuts."

David Currie lives in the same modest house he owned before he won the lottery. His phone number hasn't changed. He drives the same car. His one extravagance? An automatic garage dooropener. As for his money? He gave most of it away to his children and grandchildren, friends, his church—even some to a couple of neighborhood kids making their way through university. He's the exception, right?

Wrong. In Canada, according to Roy Kaplan, Dave is the norm. "The Canadians were far more likely to stay were they lived when they won. They didn't seem to be as obsessed with materialism as the American winners. They weren't as eager to chuck their surroundings for the idealized fantasy world. There was a very clear social net that gave support to the Canadian winners so that they were less fearful and had to spend less money on basic necessities like health care."

Canadian winners also tended to stay with their jobs—although there were some notable exceptions to that rule. Kaplan went to Rogersville, New Brunswick, to interview 14 grocery store co-workers who'd shared a

RECORD LUMP SUMS

Here is a list of some of the record lump sum cash payment jackpots handed out:

1. Illinois/ Michigan	$181.5 million	2*	May 9,2000	The Big Game
2. Indiana	$161.5 million	1	July 29, 1998	Powerball
3. Wisconsin	$104.3 million	1	May 20, 1998	Powerball
4. Minnesota	$78.9 million	1	June 30,1999	Powerball
5. U.K.	$65 million	3	Jan. 6, 1996	
6. U.K.	$62 million	4	Jan. 27, 1996	
7. Georgia	$59.1 million	1	Aug. 3, 1999	The Big Game
8. California	$51 million	3	April 18, 1998	
9. Italy	$50 million	1	Feb. 6, 1999	
10. California	$43.5 million	1	June 10, 1999	
11. Wisconsin/ Montana	$38.7 million	2	March 27, 1999	Powerball
12. Florida	$38.7 million	1	March 29, 2000	
13. Italy	$36.9 million	1	Oct. 31, 1998	
14. U.K.	$36.4 million	7	Oct. 26, 1996	
15. U.K.	$31.2 million	6	July 17, 1999	

* number of winning tickets

million dollar jackpot. When he got to the store, he found that the every one of the winners had quit. You've heard of bag-your-own? This sounds more like price, ring in, and bag-your-own.

Chapter 5

Near Misses

After picking up his $181.5 million check—his share of a record $363 million lottery jackpot—Larry Ross admitted that he almost fell prey to the lottery player's worst nightmare: he almost didn't cash his winning ticket in. It seems Ross, the owner of a pool company in Shelby, Michigan, had copied down the wrong winning numbers.

It all started when Ross went into Mr. K's Party Shoppe, a convenience store near Utica, 20 miles outside of Detroit. He bought a hot dog and handed the clerk a $100 bill, asking for his change in Big Game lottery tickets. Big Game was started in 1996 by six states: Georgia, Illinois, Maryland, Massachusetts, and Virginia. Their aim was a high-odds, big jackpot game to compete with Powerball. Originally, players had to match five out of 50 numbers, along with hitting the "Big Ball" selected out of a pool of 25. In 1999, organizers made two significant changes. First, they added New Jersey to the mix, significantly expanding their potential audience. Then they made it more difficult to hit the Big Ball, increasing the pool to 36 balls. The odds of hitting the jackpot number were now on par with Powerball: one in 76.3 million.

With the increased odds came bigger prizes, and by the year 2000, Big Game had notched two of the top ten jackpots in American history, including a $197 million pot, the second biggest win of all time. As the new millennium dawned, something happened to Big Game. On March 7, the jackpot stood at a reasonable $5 million. Over the next two months, players missed the jackpot 18 times, and by the time Larry Ross bought

CHECK, PLEASE

 If you're going to go to the trouble of buying lottery tickets, go to the trouble of checking them after the draw.

It sounds like a simple rule, but each year millions of dollars go unclaimed because people don't bother to check their tickets. In Powerball alone, 12 percent of the total prizes go unclaimed; as much as 30 percent of the smaller—that is, less than $1 million—prizes are unclaimed.

his tickets, the jackpot was well over $300 million. A new record was being set.

On the night of the draw, Larry Ross heard the winning numbers on the radio. He quickly copied them down. Later, he checked his tickets against the winners. Close, but no cigar. One of the numbers was wrong. But then, fate stepped in.

"The next morning we saw the clerk who had sold us the ticket on TV," Larry's wife Nancy explained to reporters. "We rechecked the ticket and found we had won."

In his haste, Larry had actually copied down an extra number. If they hadn't seen the convenience store clerk on TV, who knows what might have happened? They might still be poor schleps like the rest of us. How close the Ross's came to losing out was underscored seven days later when the holders of the other ticket on the winning number stepped forward. As Sue and Joe Kainz, owners of a micro brewery in Lack County, Illinois, were accepting their check, the director of the Illinois lottery was urging everyone to double check their tickets. To date, seven $150,000-winning tickets had yet to be claimed.

Unclaimed lottery prizes are a big problem. Each year, countless millions of dollars are rolled back into prize pools across North America, as hapless "winners" lose, overlook, and otherwise forget their lucky tickets. In the Powerball, for example, as many as 12 percent of winning tickets go unclaimed. What lotteries do with unclaimed prize money varies from state to state: some return it to players in the form of bonus draws, others throw it into general revenue.

How can lottery players come so close, only to let a jackpot slip from their hands? According to Esther French, it's not as hard as it sounds. She

THE STATE OF COMMISSIONS

George Kassab, owner of Mr. K's Party Shoppe, got a $2,000 bonus for selling Larry Ross his record-breaking lottery ticket. Not bad, you say. But consider the case of John Sweeney, a gas station owner in Lake Zurick, a Chicago suburb. For selling Sue and Joe Kainz their winning ticket, he took home a check for $1.8 million. The difference? The Illinois Lottery gives sellers a 1 percent commission on winning tickets, while the Michigan Lottery only offers a flat fee.

isn't normally forgetful, she just got so busy that the lottery ticket slipped her mind.

"It all started with my feet," Esther told us. "I was having trouble with them and I needed orthotics."

Her husband Bill worked at Stelco in Hamilton, Ontario, where he had extra medical coverage, so it was just a simple matter of him bringing home some insurance papers and the orthotics were hers.

"Thursday when he came home from work he was supposed to bring the papers home with him, but forgot. So he went into work early Friday morning to pick them up. On the way, he went into the bank; he was supposed to get money out, then he changed his mind. He thought he'd go into work first, then get the money on the way home. He stopped off for coffee and bought a quick pick, and then went to work and got the forms. Then he came home and gave me the forms as well as the ticket."

Bill has his routine when it comes to buying tickets for Lotto 6/49, Canada's national lottery run by a collection of provincial lottery agencies. He plays two special sets of numbers, one based on important family dates like birthdays and anniversaries, and the other based on his parent's special dates. He also buys two quick picks every week: one for Esther, and one for her mom. But on this day he ignored his usual pattern and bought another quick pick on a whim. That was August 27, 1994. The next day, the day of the draw, the French's started off on a holiday trip to a little town in Newfoundland called Rose-Blanche Petite.

"I put the ticket in a little brag album I was fixing up with pictures of all the grandchildren, to take with us to show friends we met along the way. I just carried this around with us all the time we were away."

It's a 24-hour drive from Hamilton, Ontario, to Sydney, Nova Scotia, where Esther and Bill planned to catch the ferry to Newfoundland. They didn't have a chance to check their ticket along the way, so when they got to Sydney they looked for a lottery store. They couldn't find one. "We figured it was no big deal, and continued on our holiday."

When she got back from her trip, Esther stuck the ticket on the fridge under a magnet. And there it sat. And sat. "I kept saying to Bill every now and again, 'How about checking that ticket out?' But he never did."

Finally, one month after the draw, the French's got around to looking at their ticket. Bill picked up a list of winning numbers at a corner store and brought it home. "We were sitting around the kitchen table and I was showing my dad some pictures of the holidays, and Bill was going through checking a number of tickets that he had around the house."

Esther could see Bill out of the corner of her eye; he kept going over one particular ticket. He checked three or four times before passing it to Esther.

"Is this a ticket?" Bill asked her, thinking that maybe he was just looking at a print-out of a winning number—or maybe someone was playing a joke?

"Well, you paid a dollar for it, didn't you?" Esther replied.

Bill insisted that Esther check it out, so she took a good, long look at the ticket. "Looks like it's a good winner, honey," she said nonchalantly.

Esther recalls that at the time, she didn't know how much they had won. "We had all six numbers, so we knew it would probably be a fair amout of money. But it didn't really hit me at all; it was just a winner, that was it."

Still not completely convinced, Bill went down to the corner store and asked the clerk to check the ticket for him. The clerk said that if he checked the ticket and it was a winner, he'd have to pay it out. "You won't be paying this one out," Bill replied.

The computer confirmed the truth that Bill could not bring himself to believe. He and his wife were millionaires.

"I was very calm about it all," Esther recalls. "It didn't phase me. But Bill, I could see him getting more agitated. He kept pacing and pacing. In the thirty-two years that we've been married, I've never seen him pace."

After a sleepless night, Bill and Esther drove to the lottery office in Toronto 45 minutes away. Their son Randy—a musician, who along with Steve Holick, performs in an Irish-inspired band, the *Celtic Cowboys*—came along for the ride.

"You hear horror stories. So you think you're going to be mugged, there's going to be people waiting there to grab your money the moment you walk out of the lottery office. So we had our son Randy come with us. Actually, we had to have him drive because my husband was just so on edge and preoccupied that he wouldn't have been a safe driver."

THE BAD LUCK OF THE DRAW

There's near misses . . . and then there's big misses. And Clarence Jackson can tell you, they aren't pretty.

In 1995, this Hamden, Connecticut store cleaner bought ten tickets on the state lottery, then he gave them to his bedridden father to check. It was a routine they had established over the years. But this time, something went terribly wrong. Jackson's father, who was ill and had been in and out of the hospital, didn't check the ticket.

Fast forward to a year later, when Jackson's sister Sheila Cole was watching the news on TV. She saw a report on a $5.8 million jackpot that had gone unclaimed for almost a year. Cole had a funny feeling the ticket belonged to her brother. She went to her father's house and found the winning ticket tucked away in a pile. But by now it was 11:15 on a Sunday night; the year-old ticket would expire in 45 minutes. Had she known, she could have taken the ticket to be validated at any store that sold lottery tickets. Instead, Cole believed she had to bring it to the lottery office to collect. She watched the 45 minutes tick by, and the ticket transform into just another worthless piece of paper. But there may be light at the end of the tunnel. State legislators have taken up the cause, and Jackson remains patently optimistic.

All their worry was in vain, though. There wasn't a crowd of muggers waiting to greet them at the lottery centre; there wasn't even a reporter. They did, however, get the red carpet treatment from the lottery people.

"They gave us a royal welcome. They brought us into another room, and told us to sit down and relax. I think they understand how people are nervous about what they're coming up against. Most people aren't in that situation very often, so you don't know how to cope with it. The lottery people are really very attentive and help put you at ease."

Bill and Esther, who shared their winning set of numbers with a family from Quebec, left the lottery office with a check for exactly $1,064,190.40 ("We gave my son-in-law the forty cents," Esther jokes). From there, they drove straight to their bank and handed the check over to the manager.

"He was very surprised, very happy for us. He was willing to negotiate paying our mortgage off with no penalty, if we were willing to invest the money all there. We had other ideas. But there was no problem; we worked everything out."

DON'T HOLD YOUR BREATH

If you buy one ticket a week on a 6/49-style draw, you can expect to win the jackpot once every 134,460 years, and claim a second place prize once every 533 years.

They paid their mortgage off right then and there, cleared up a few other bills, then had the bank draw up some checks for numerous relatives. "One hour later, we were no longer millionaires," Esther quipped. "But it was nice getting out of debt. To me, the best thing about it all was that my husband was able to retire, and now we can do things together. We used to go to Niagara Falls maybe once a year on our anniversary to get away and have a break. Now, it's nice to be able to just head out the door with our bags, not knowing when we will be back."

With the mortgage paid off, and the balance of their windfall safely invested and banked away, Esther finally had time to relax. And that's when the enormity of the event sunk in.

"Two weeks after we won, I woke up in the middle of the night in a cold sweat wondering what the hell was going on. Then I realised that we had no more debt. I'd been looking after the books for some time, and we've been going from pay to pay, robbing Peter to pay Paul. But we always had the attitude, if we have to sell the house we'll sell the house. At least we'll have each other. We enjoyed ourselves along the way, in debt or not."

Now that all is said and done, does Esther ever look back and wonder what life would be like if she hadn't remembered her forgotten ticket?

"Oh, yes. But what you don't know can't hurt you. And if we had lost it, we would have still been in debt, that's all; there just wouldn't have been any surprises."

For a lot of people, it seems that getting the right numbers is the second hardest thing about winning the lottery. The hardest is hanging onto the ticket.

Consider the case of Harold Reid. In May 1997, this New York City taxi driver won $7.6 million on the state lottery. The only catch? He'd accidentally thrown his winning ticket in the trash. He did, however, have his receipt showing the winning numbers: 8, 41, 49, 52, 53, 54. Did he get his money? You bet. But only after spending three years in court battling the New York Lottery.

Gary Querel is one person whose memory lapse almost cost a bundle. Today, Gary owns his own auto-body repair business. He's also a world champion snowmobile racer, competing in up to 50 competitions a year. But in January 1977, he was just a kid out of high school, unsure of his future.

"My mom would buy us each a ticket for every draw. She'd also check the ticket for us. It's a good system when you're eighteen years old," Gary said in a phone interview from his home in Winnipeg.

Rita Querel had bought her son a ticket on the December 29 draw; on December 28, she and her husband left for a Hawaiian vacation, leaving Gary and his brother George home alone. Gary put the ticket on top of the television and forgot about it. It sat there unnoticed for two weeks.

"One night I was talking to my girlfriend on the phone and I just happened to pick the ticket up. I said, 'Hey, I just found an old lottery ticket here, I wonder if won?'"

Gary read the number to his girlfriend, who checked it in the paper. "She told me it was good for $50,000. I didn't really believe her. So I called the lottery office. She *was* wrong. I'd actually won $100,000." Ten minutes later, Gary was at the lottery office collecting his check, as his parents were, coincidentally, jetting their way back to Winnipeg.

So what does a teenager do with all that money?

Like a good son, Gary gave some to his parents, and put a chunk of it in the bank. And of course, for a kid whose passion was snowmobile racing, he did allow himself one treat.

"The big thing was I took a trip down to California with a couple of buddies of mine. We had a great time, and I splurged and bought a custom-made leather racing suit that cost about $3,500. Sure, it was expensive, but it was the best suit around, and that's what lotteries are for, right?"

A Washington, D.C. security guard found out that it pays to check those pockets. Ronnie Solomon Ware, Sr. was carrying a pocketful of lottery tickets for a week before he decided to check his numbers. Turns out he was holding a big winner on an April 1996 Powerball lottery. Ware shared a $34 million jackpot with another ticket holder—although he lost out on several thousand dollars' worth of interest on the overlooked ticket.

Canadians waited eight months once to find out who had become the latest millionaire in Lotto 6/49.

The draw was held October 25, 1986. Lottery officials knew that someone had the winning ticket; their computer records showed that it had been purchased from a Royal Canadian Legion in Winnipeg. But time

---

BEST LAID PLANS

If you won a million bucks on the lottery, would you know what to do with it? We asked our resident financial advisor for some tips:

1. **Move.** That's right. If you win big—say, $3 million—the smartest financial move you could make would be to move to a tax haven country like the Bahamas. This way the money you make from investing your winnings will be taxed at a much lower rate than it would be at home.

2. **Divide and conquer.** So you just can't leave the land of the free for the land of the tax-free? Then expect to pay an income tax rate of close to 40 percent on your investment income. You might be able to move into a lower tax bracket, though, if you divide your winnings among family and friends. Husbands and wives, for example, often claim winning tickets jointly, and have both their names on their jackpot checks. The less money one person has, the lower their investment return—and as far as tax is concerned, less is more.

3. **Take the money and run.** In other words, don't delay. On a multi-million dollar win, you could lose thousands of dollars in interest by waiting even just a few days to collect.

4. **Go crazy.** If you really don't want to pay tax, buy a whole bunch of stuff. Get a house or two for yourself, and one each for your kids,

---

passed, and passed, and no one stepped forward to claim the $2.2 million prize.

In January 1987, rumors spread that a winner was about to step forward. Apparently, a chiropractor held the lucky ticket, but was keeping it a secret for his own mysterious reasons. A reporter from the *Winnipeg Free Press* tracked down the apparent winner, a Dr. Peter Palaschuk.

"I wish it was true," Palaschuk told the reporter. The doctor went on to say that he'd been hounded by people who'd heard the rumor of his windfall. "It's ridiculous. I'm not keeping it a secret. I didn't win. Let the people know that the winning ticket is still out there."

Six months later, Eugene Uhryniuk, a graduate student at the University of Manitoba, was cleaning out some old books at the end of the semester. He came across on a textbook on international relations. When he opened it up, there was a surprise waiting.

"I knew I'd won, but I thought I'd lost the ticket," he told the press conference. "Initially, I was in shock. I thought, 'This couldn't be happening to me.'"

parents, and in-laws. You'll only pay tax on interest or other invest ment earnings, so the less actual cash you have left to squirrel away, the better off you'll be when the tax man comes a-knocking.

5. **Seek shelter.** At your own risk, that is. Most tax shelters mean you pay the tax shelter people the money you would have otherwise paid to the government. And if someone offers you a guaranteed return for investing in their next motion picture—don't believe it. You probably won't see your money again; but hey, that's show business.

6. **Be selective.** Choose your friends—and financial advisers—wisely. Don't pick a financial adviser out of the phone book. Get someone you know and trust to recommend their stockbroker or accountant. If you feel uncomfortable at all upon meeting them, try someone else.

7. **Be wary of subscription services.** There's nothing life-threatening about Lotto Advance or other prepayment services, but if you do happen to win, there is a computer record of who bought the tick et. That means that you can't go halvsies with your spouse after the fact. Not that you would.

8. **Give generously.** You can give 20 percent of your net income to reg istered charities and get a full deduction.

Eugene, then 24, planned to use the money to buy a nice car, and to take a year off from his studies to concentrate on his musical career. But was he upset that because of the eight-month delay he'd lost $100,000 in interest?

"I prefer to take a different view; I was lucky to find the ticket."

You can say that again, Eugene.

Fate must have been watching out for Bill McLaughlin. In July 1978, the Vancouver postal clerk was offered a *Western Express* ticket at a charity bingo.

"Funny thing was, I didn't take the ticket booklet I was offered," Bill told reporters. "I dug around and picked out one from the bottom of the pile."

And after he bought the ticket? He put it in his wallet and forgot about it until he went in to work a few days later. "When I arrived at work a buddy said, 'Guess you didn't win the big one because you turned up today.'"

That was all it took to twig Bill's memory. At lunch he checked the *Vancouver Sun* for winning ticket numbers. "There was my ticket—0910229. I'm still shaking. I hadn't looked at my ticket once until today."

Don't you hate moving day?

For six Mississauga office clerks, moving day nearly cost them dearly. In February, 1983, the co-workers bought a $10 SuperLotto ticket, and left it in the care of Arlene Johnson. "Arlene put it in her briefcase and we forgot about it when the company moved," Margaret Ford, one of the clerks, told reporters.

Two months later, Arlene was going through her briefcase when she discovered the ticket. "She gave it to Anne McMahon to check the number and, before you knew it, Anne was screaming all over the office." The misplaced ticket turned out to be a $1 million winner, which amounted to $166,666.67 for each member of the pool. Maybe moving day isn't so bad after all.

Like father, like son? Well, not all the time. And it was a good thing, too, at least for William Rogers, whose son paid better attention to lottery tickets than he did.

In November, 1986, William and his wife took a little trip from their home in Seattle. They drove north to Vancouver, and on their way home stopped at the Ocean Park Smoke and Gift Shop in Surrey, B.C., where they bought a Lotto 6/49 ticket. The thing is, he never bothered to check later on to see if he had the winning number.

Two months later, William's son Richard was in the library and decided to check through back issues of the *Vancouver Sun* to see if his father's number had come up. It had, to the tune of $1.8 million.

Julius Russell may just have the greatest lost and found story of all . . . make that, the greatest lost and *not* found story.

Julius, a 60 year old janitor from Chicago, didn't claim his winning ticket for a full year, and then asked the Illinois State Lottery to take his word for it. You see, he didn't have the actual ticket. But he distinctly remembered buying it.

The story began to unfold in July 1988, when Julius' daughter Julie saw a familiar set of lottery numbers in the paper, in a story about an unclaimed jackpot.

Julie recognised the numbers—4, 14, 16, 29, 37, 41—because they were the same ones her father played every week. She showed the article to her father, who screamed "Oh my god!" then frantically searched for the year-old ticket. But alas, he couldn't find it. Not easily deterred, Julius claimed the jackpot anyway.

Of course, the lottery corporation turned him down—along with 22 other ticketless people who also filed claims. So Julius went to court, armed with a year's worth of lottery tickets, all bearing the winning numbers (and all purchased *after* the win date) and the sincere declaration that he had bought his lost ticket at the same store where, according to lottery officials, the winning ticket was bought.

The judged laughed Julius out of court, right?

Wrong.

To the resounding protests of lottery officials, the judge awarded the jackpot—$3 million plus interest—to Julius Russell. He undoubtedly laughed all the way to the bank.

CHAPTER 6

GOOD NEWS, BAD NEWS

The good news is you won the lottery. The bad news? Well, that may just be that you won the lottery.

We all like to hear stories about lottery winners. It gives us confidence in the game system, and allows us to dream of future fortunes for ourselves. But when it comes to tales of lottery losers—people who seem worse off after their wins than before—we just can't get enough.

Why? Maybe these bad news stories strike a collective nerve; we're still not completely comfortable with the idea of lotteries, where million dollar jackpots undermine everything we've ever heard about the work ethic. People should work hard to earn their rewards, not just have everything handed to them on a platter. Lotteries have led us into temptation, and left us standing on shaky moral ground. The occasional lottery loser lets us all breathe a little easier; they're a sort of sacrificial lamb who pays so the rest of us can play.

For example, remember Buddy Post? If the name sounds familiar, it's because Post won a $16 million jackpot on the Pennsylvania State Lottery in 1988. That made him famous for a little while. But what really caught people's attention were the problems that plagued Post after his win. First was his landlord, who claimed she'd split the cost of the winning ticket with the fiftyish ex-cook and carnival worker. She sued for half the jackpot, but only got one-third of it. Next up was the little matter of a jealous brother. It seems Jeffrey Post had a plan for getting his hands on some of Buddy's booty; all he had to do was find someone to bump his brother off.

"LA DOLCE VITA"

You'd think that Jimmy Cohoon's $500,000, 11-month spending spree would stand as something of a record in the Lottery Hall of Fame, but alas, Cohoon had barely made his last withdrawal when someone came along and took the Biggest Spendthrift title right from under his nose.

The new record holder was a softspoken man from Yellowknife with the unlikely name of Henry Squirrel. In April 1985, the unemployed father of three came across a free ticket on the Provincial Lottery. A few days later, his number came up, and Squirrel found himself $500,000 richer. Overnight, the 60 year old went from living on the streets to sleeping in $250-a-night hotel suites.

Over the next few months, Squirrel spent his money on friends, family, women, and "the good life." He even invested some of it, putting a $38,000 down payment on an apartment building in Vancouver; the only problem was, he promptly forgot the address, and was never able to track it down. As for the woman who arranged this real estate transaction, Squirrel gave her a $15,000 car for her trouble because she never asked him for a handout.

Because of his friendly nature, Squirrel was an easy mark. He claimed to have been robbed half a dozen times after his windfall, one time losing over $8,000. In late August he befriended a woman who turned around and robbed him of $15,000—which, by the way, was the last of his money. In barely four months, Henry Squirrel had gone through half a million dollars.

"I tried to spend this money the way I felt like doing," Squirrel told a reporter at that time. "Now I have the experience and know what happens with this kind of money."

And if he won again? Well, next time around, Squirrel swore, he would invest it all.

Fortunately, the police arrested Jeffrey before he could put his plan into action.

Buddy himself wasn't above the odd run-in with the law. In 1991, after his bar and used car businesses had gone belly up, Buddy was having a financial discussion with his stepdaughter's boyfriend. The discussion ended with Post firing a gun into the air to, as he later explained, scare the young man off. Post was arrested and sentenced to six months in jail—although appeals kept him out of the slammer. Two years after the incident, Post filed for bankruptcy. He owed more than half a million dollars—not including back taxes and lawyers' fees. The last we heard of Buddy, he was living in his mansion with no heat or electricity—he couldn't pay the bills—trying to flog the last 17 installments of his lottery windfall. But even that ointment had its own particular fly in it. Pennsylvania Lottery officials were trying to block any potential sale, stating that a winner had no right to sell off future lottery payments. You'd think they'd be happy to let Buddy do it, just to get his name out of the papers.

Buddy Post's story is just one example of the darker side of the lotteries. But perhaps the most famous of all lottery losers is James "Jimmy" Cohoon, a seaman whose rags-to-riches-to-rags story captivated the imagination of millions in the late 1980s. In September 1984, Cohoon was working as night-watchman on the Atlantic Superior, a ship at that time in dry dock in Thunder Bay, Ontario. He'd been at the job for seven months, and had spent most of his life working on or around the water.

"I started fishing when I was fifteen down in Canso, Nova Scotia," James says. "Since then I've worked the ships, off the coast and on the lakes. You ask me if I like being on the water, and to tell you the truth, I think I'm hooked on it. And the older you get, the worse you get. When I go to shore now, if I'm not drinking, I'm watching that clock go. I can't get back on the ship quick enough."

Like lots of seamen, James liked to drink—he never made any bones about that—and he also liked to play the lottery, particularly the Provincial. "I played any lottery game, if I wasn't drinking. At that time, see, I had a good job on a deep sea ship, and I hadn't drank for two and a half years. I was doing good until I won that."

James had 60 Provincial tickets, $300 worth, for the September 21 draw. He was sitting in his friend's house the next day when he remembered his tickets.

"While we were in the kitchen talking, I said, 'Did you get the numbers for that Provincial last night? I might have won something.' So he gave me the numbers, and I started checking through them. But I didn't have nothing. Then my friend's son, who must have been twelve or thirteen years old, said, 'Dad, you didn't tell him right. You didn't give him the right numbers.' And he got the paper. . . ."

James read the correct numbers in the paper, then checked his tickets again. As he went through his tickets one by one, Cohoon almost fell off his chair. The seven-digit number on one ticket matched the number in the paper. He'd won himself half a million dollars.

"I might have thrown the tickets away if I hadn't double-checked, I suppose. But you used to get five draws; you know, the tickets were good for five weeks. That ticket was good for a couple more weeks; I don't think I would have thrown that one away. I would have checked the next week."

The next day, he quit his job and headed to Toronto with his friend to collect his winnings. That's where the story ends and the legend begins. Cohoon put his money in the bank, then immediately withdrew $100,000 cash. He gave half of that to his buddy from Thunder Bay, then after stopping for a few cocktails, high-tailed it to Toronto's Moss Park, a hang-out for drunks and the homeless. Before the afternoon was done, Cohoon had gone through his cash. "I was doing all right, but when I hit the booze—game over."

Originally, James had big plans for his money. He'd hoped to go to Ireland, his ancestral homeland, and wanted to buy a fishing boat. He even bought himself a $200,000 bond, to make sure he had some savings left over when the partying was finished. But when he headed back to Halifax, everything fell apart. He got a room in a nice hotel, and spent most of the day at bars like Ginger's Tavern. When he wasn't tossing back beers, he was wandering the back roads and streets handing out tens, twenties, fifties, and more. It wasn't beyond him to leave a $100 tip for his favorite waitress, and once, out of the blue, handed a $1,000 bill to a skid row prostitute.

"She said she'd never seen one before in her life," Cohoon told a reporter about the G-note gift. "The girl had her picture taken with it. It made her happy for one night."

Then there was the time Cohoon climbed to the top floor of the Scotia Square with a bag of twenties and started pitching bills to the startled shoppers below.

Cohoon bought cars for five of his pals, including a Cadillac that his buddy Blackie chauffeured him around the Maritimes in for a few weeks. He gave another friend, Ron Pottie, $110,000 to buy a house; James says that he was supposed to have an apartment in the house for the rest of his life, although he still hasn't seen it.

"When I got down amongst me friends and I got drinking, I didn't care about the $500,000; I thought there would never be no end to that. I figured, why worry about yourself when you've got a buzz on and half a million dollars in the bank?"

But the most famous story of all was the time Cohoon and his pal Bun Hubley caught a cab outside a bank. Cohoon, who'd just made a withdrawal, got an idea.

"Can you keep your mouth shut?" he asked the cab driver.

The driver shrugged and nodded. Cohoon looked around cautiously, then lowered his voice.

"We just robbed a bank," Cohoon continued, and lifted up his shirt to reveal a bundle a cash. Needless to say, the driver ditched his passengers as soon as possible, and never even thanked them for their $20 tip.

James saw the end coming. He was in Sydney, on Cape Breton, and his bank account was dwindling.

"I think I had $7,000 left when I came to Halifax. I got $5,000 the first day, and I gave $3,000 to an old girlfriend who said she wanted to buy a car, but I know she didn't. And then, I only had $2,000 left, so I was only getting out a few dollars a day."

Exactly 11 months after collecting his windfall, James Cohoon walked into his bank and filled out a withdrawal slip.

"I'm sorry, sir," the teller said, "but this account is empty."

Cohoon scratched his head, then shuffled out of the bank. He scraped through his pockets, and added up the bills and coins; he now had $11 left from his half million. He had dinner that night at Hope Cottage, the Roman Catholic mission, but he disputes the widely reported story that he spent the night on a park bench.

"I slept on a friend's couch. I never really did sleep in the streets."

Over the next few weeks Cohoon called on all his fast-times friends, his hat in hand. But their gratitude had faded like yesterday's hangover, and one by one they closed their doors on their former friend. Cohoon tried to be philosophical.

"You don't regret," he told the press. "I would have done it different if I hadn't been drinking so much."

At one time, Cohoon's story would have ended here. But in this fallen land of lotteries, the press didn't even notice James until he'd hit bottom again, and then they froze that moment in time. Papers across the country carried in-depth interviews with Cohoon, his friends, and his family, playing up his rampant generosity and down-playing the underlying cause. Despite what you've read, James wasn't a happy-go-lucky bum: he was normally a hard-working man with an alcohol problem.

What the press doesn't tell you is that Cohoon was back working on a ship by Christmas. Today, he says he resents being painted as a bum and a con artist—and believes most of the reporters he's talked to over the years were only interested in telling their version of the truth, not his.

"I was five years on the one ship, thirteen years with one company; the way they've got the story there, it's like I was on the bum all me life. I've got over one hundred discharges, which are registered up in Ottawa; how could I be a bum and a con artist, and still do all that work?"

When I last spoke with Cohoon, he was working on board the *A.E. Farquharson* in the Great Lakes, a job he has held since 1988. "Now I work half a year because it's frozen over the rest of the time. But when I was down on the coast, I worked all winter in the deep sea. And when I first joined this one, we worked three months on and got one month off. Now we're up on the Great Lakes, it's different."

James says he still plays lotteries, although he hopes he'd be a little more conservative if he won the jackpot again. But when you get right down to it, he has more practical concerns on his mind than how to spend the next lottery check.

"Things are working out pretty good for me now. I'll just hang in there until I'm sixty-five, then if the government's got any money left, I'll get my pension, and maybe work part-time 'til I can't work any more."

"I wouldn't wish this on anybody," Bob Campbell of Sault St. Marie, Ontario told reporters in March 1988. What particular horror was he describing? A 30-car pile-up? A root canal? A tax audit? Waxy yellow buildup on his kitchen floors?

Nope. Campbell was talking about the $6.4 million he won on Lotto 6/49 in 1986.

"I'm far from broke. I can last three or four lifetimes with what I've got. I'm not going to give it away, but I would be just as happy without it."

Campbell, who was 27 when he hit the jackpot, is one of the lucky ones; nothing particularly unpleasant happened to him, it's just that after his win, the rest of his life seemed anti-climactic.

"The only hope or dream I ever had was to win a lot of money in a lottery," Campbell told the press at the time. "I've done that."

For those seeking a cautionary tale about the lottery, look no further than Mike Allen. On Christmas Eve 1988, Allen won almost $6 million on the Megabucks lottery. Within six weeks of getting his first installment, worth about $220,000, the money was gone. He gave a portion each to his mother, sister, and brother; the rest he squandered on new-found friends. In less than ten years, Allen was bankrupt, and was forced to sell the rest of his annuity to pay off his debts. Less than a year later, he was found in his apartment, his face hammered beyond recognition. He'd been murdered by one of his tenants, putting an end to an incredible string of bad luck that had been set in motion by his lottery win.

When Joe Kulnyo, 44, won his jackpot of $364,000 in 1985, he couldn't even afford to go get it. At the time, he was out of work and living at the

YMCA in Regina, and had to borrow $500 to fly to Winnipeg in order to collect his check. A native of Hungary who had emigrated to Canada 28 years earlier, Joe had been a steelworker, hotel clerk, and security guard, but because of his alcoholism, could never hold a job for very long.

The win brought—or perhaps more aptly, bought—Joe a new group of friends, who encouraged him to drink up and, by all means, pick up the tab. And while Joe was away in Hungary seeing his parents for the first time since he left home, his new friends pawned everything he owned.

Joe's drinking got worse, to the point where he checked himself into a detox center. But it was too late. He stayed off the bottle for only ten days. He started having seizures whenever he stopped drinking. Six days later, the police found Joe in a back lane. He'd drank two bottles of vodka and passed out face-first in a mud puddle. He drowned in less than an inch of water.

Like Joe Kuknyo, Gerald Roberts had to borrow money to collect his lottery jackpot. In 1977, Roberts won Loto-Canada, making him Newfoundland's first lottery millionaire. At first, though, the "hobo" couldn't even get a bank loan to fly to Montreal to pick up his winnings.

Eventually, he did collect, and went on a spending spree, buying a car for each of his 12 closest friends, and partying for an entire month in some of St. John's finest bars and lounges. He also spent $300,000 on a luxury yacht—"a pleasure palace," in the words of one lottery official—that attracted babes and booze.

One year to the day after winning his prize, Roberts died after learning that the money was all gone.

Arnold High is another who would have been better off without the lottery. In March 1990, Calgary's High won $1 million in the Provincial. Days later, the 84-year-old was hauled into court by his longtime companion, a 37-year-old nurse, who demanded half of the jackpot. The judge seized the money for the duration of the trial, but eight weeks later, Harold High died without ever spending a penny of his windfall.

"The winning of the money was the worst thing that could have happened to him," son Harold High said at the time. "It made it bad for him. We noticed ourselves how fast he went downhill."

Sometimes it's better just to take the money and run.

That's what the Stacey family of Smithers, B.C. decided after winning a share of one of Canada's biggest-ever lottery jackpots.

In October of 1993, builder Garry Stacey and five co-workers chipped in to buy 30 Lotto 6/49 tickets. To their disbelief, their number came up and the builders found themselves sharing $15 million. The winners made a quick trip 500 miles south to Vancouver to pick up their checks, and even joined the pop group the Barenaked Ladies on stage for an impromptu performance of the hit "If I Had a Million Dollars."

At the time, Garry Stacey assured the press that the money would not affect his lifestyle. "There's no way a bunch of hard workers like us are going to let our hands get as soft as our butts. There's no better place than Smithers."

Seven months later, they were telling the press that they'd had enough of life in the gilded cage. "It's brought a lot of stress to the family," Garry's wife Kris told the *Vancouver Sun*. "The phone calls, the rumors. And being in a small town, it's hard to go out anywhere. It's hard to know how much to tip without being called a cheapskate."

At last report, the Staceys had sold their house and were planning to relocate somewhere in B.C. after taking a year off in Australia. "Before we won, we worked hard for what little we had. People forget that."

Within a few years of winning $1 million on the Provincial, Robert and Kelly Maxwell had lost it all on a string of bad investments. But they're not singing the blues. In fact, they think they're better off as honest working folk than as instant millionaires.

Kelly Maxwell gets downright philosophical when she talks about her short-lived lavish lifestyle. "If you work for your money and lose it, that's very, very sad. But if you don't work for your money and you lose it, that's okay, because that's the way you were meant to be."

The Maxwells scored their jackpot in 1979, but lost it all in the recession of the early 1980s. Within four years, they were living on a rented eight-acre farm in British Columbia's beautiful Pemberton Valley, 120 miles north of Vancouver. Kelly was working winters at a ski hill, while Robert drove a dump truck six days a week to make ends meet.

"We're not meant to be rich," Kelly concluded in an interview with the *Vancouver Sun*. "We never were."

Too bad Montreal's Barbara Bailey didn't talk to a financial planner after she won a $1.2 million Lotto 6/49 jackpot in 1989.

She seemed to start off on the right foot. One of the first things Barbara did was to buy a house; not an opulent mansion, but a nice, pleasant house in the $200,000 range.

She enjoyed living the life of a millionaire and took great delight in loaning her wealth to friends and relatives—or flat-out giving it away.

AFFLUENZA

 Have you found that you just haven't been yourself since you won that million dollar lottery? Don't worry, you've probably just got a touch of "affluenza"—what some psychologists are calling the emotional distress that often follows a windfall like a lottery win. Now, there's a disease we wouldn't mind catching.

Also know as Sudden Wealth Syndrome, psychologists say it's characterized by feelings of guilt, alienation, fear, and uncertainty. How to avoid affluenza? While there are no hard and fast rules, simple common sense dictates that you should take your time before making any decisions about your newly-aquired wealth. A lot of winners have also found that performing charity work helps ease their mind. It also helps to make a budget and stick to it, in order to avoid the feeling that your money is slowly slipping away. Most of all, a positive attitude can make a world of difference. Believe in yourself, that you're worthy of the windfall, and don't let anyone convince you that your money can't make a difference in the world.

Within two years she was broke, and turned to her bank for some help—or rather, she helped herself to some of the bank's money. She enlisted the help of her niece, a teller who diverted money from term deposit accounts and into her aunt's pocket. Over time, Barbara milked Lloyd's Bank of $500,000 to help maintain her high-roller image.

It didn't take the bank long to catch on to the scam. Barbara was arrested and charged with possession of stolen property. The judge gave her two years.

"She played . . . only to wind up on welfare, in the care of citizens," the judge told the court. "This is not a case deserving sympathy."

Anthony Carrato may just be the unluckiest lottery winner ever. When he won half a million dollars in a Loto Canada draw, it was as if he stepped out of this dimension and entered the Twilight Zone.

"All the fanfare of winning was replaced with weights on my shoulders," Carrato told a reporter a few years after his nightmare win.

When the story began, the Buffalo, New York native seemed on top of the world. It was October 9, 1977, and Carrato and his wife had just

CASH FOR LIFER

 Convicted arsonist Richard Costa picked a hot ticket, and won $1,000-a-month-for-life on Pennsylvania's lottery. The state demanded that part of the money go towards repaying his victims and court costs.

split a million dollar Canadian jackpot with Anna Pecoraro, his mother-in-law. One month later, Carrato got a bill from the Internal Revenue Service, and all of a sudden his windfall just looked like a lot of wind. In those days, $500,000 Canadian was worth about $450,000 U.S.; Uncle Sam presented Carrato with a $308,000 U.S. tax bill (even though the lottery is tax-free in Canada, American winners still have to ante up to their own government). On top of that, New York demanded $63,000 U.S. in state taxes. When all was said and done, Carrato would have been left with $80,000.

The operative phrase is "would have." Carrato decided—IRS be damned—that he would keep his winnings. He and his wife left town, and after a five-week Latin American vacation, they bought a house in Niagara Falls, Ontario, and applied for landed residence status in Canada. Soon they opened a coin shop in the Honeymoon Capital of the World, and settled into what they thought was the good life. Their only bother was the occasional threatening letter from the IRS.

The Carratos might have lived happily ever after, until Anthony began feeling a little homesick. In January 1982, on Anthony's way back to the U.S., a customs officer stopped him at the American border and, after a routine computer check, arrested him. He spent the next two months in jail.

Believe it or not, things got worse for Carrato after he was released on $100,000 bail. He lost his coin shop; first it was raided by an American receiver, with the approval of the Canadian courts, then the banks picked through whatever was left to make up for the loans he defaulted on while in jail. And by January 1884, his IRS bill, including back taxes and penalties, was over $620,000 U.S.

"They don't really want any money from me," Carrato said at the time. "They want to crush me, that's all. They want to use me as an example to scare people into paying their taxes."

Of course, he never played the lottery again. . . .

Just kidding. Carrato kept at it, hoping that once again he would defy the odds in the luck of the draw. Except this time, he hoped, he would wind up on the other side of the Twilight Zone.

DON'T WORRY, BE HAPPY

Worried that unwanted publicity is going to ruin your next 6/49 jackpot? Don't. Unless you win a huge amount of money—$5 million at least—the press isn't interested. And most winners, even those who receive giant jackpots, are rarely bothered by money-grubbers or scam artists (who have all, apparently, gone to work for the banks).

Still, you're modest by nature, and would prefer to keep the media out of your hair.

Well, technically, you don't have much say. The lottery companies get a one-time use of your name and photograph for publicity purposes, although the old Loto Canada allowed folks to collect "in trust," and thus remain anonymous. Having said all that, there just might be a way around the publicity problem.

Herman Deschenes was only 23 when he won $1 million on Super Loto in 1980, but he showed the savvy of someone much older. When it came time to collect his check, the young man from a small town in the Gaspé region of Quebec sent his lawyer, and refused to have his photo taken. Loto-Quebec told him to "say cheese" or they'd stop payment; Deschenes told them to "say uncle" or he'd launch a publicity campaign of his own.

Moreover, Deschenes hadn't let the seller put an i.d. number on the ticket. If Loto-Quebec didn't back off, Deschenes threatened to tell every ticket dealer in town that they were entitled to the $10,000 commission for selling the winning ticket. In the end, Deschenes proved that you can get one over on the lottery companies.

"They had lots of trouble with me," he told a reporter from the *Montreal Gazette* a few years after the dust had settled. "They made me sign many papers, but I made them sign, too."

CHAPTER 7

FAMILY

It's not always true that the family who plays together stays together. Consider the trials and tribulations of Canada's Lavigueur family—truly one of the most unusual stories in lotto history.

It all started one lazy Sunday afternoon late in March, 1986, when an unemployed man named Bill Murphy was making his rounds through the streets of Montreal. He'd been out of work for some time, and lived off welfare in a cheap rooming house in the Westmount district. Sometimes, to earn a little extra money, Murphy would deliver flyers door-to-door, and on this day he came across a wallet lying in the middle of the road.

He stuck the wallet in his pocket with every intention of returning it to its rightful owner. Who knows? He thought they might even give him a reward.

When he peeked inside, he found six lottery tickets. Now, Murphy was an honest man—more honest than most—but he decided to keep the unsigned Lotto 6/49 tickets for himself. Times were tough; maybe one of them would win him a couple of bucks. But the wallet? No, he wouldn't keep that. He stuck it in a mailbox, hoping it would find its way home.

That night, the 28-year-old Murphy sat in a coffee shop and checked the numbers. A moment later, he realized that he was holding a $7.6 million jackpot winner in his hand.

"I almost had a heart attack," Murphy explained to the press at the time. "For about two hours I thought of keeping all the money to myself.

If you had a piece of paper worth almost $8 million, would you be thinking rationally?"

Murphy racked his brain. He remembered the guy's name—Lavigueur—but what was the address? Somewhere on Logan Street, he thought. Murphy set off to the East End to try and track down the real winner.

Meanwhile, Jean Guy Lavigueur had no idea of the drama that was unfolding. He had problems of his own. He lost his job at the United Bedding mattress factory months before, and his unemployment benefits had just ran out. Now, the widowed father of three was about to go on welfare. On top of everything else, he'd lost his wallet. The way things were going, he didn't even consider that the family's missing lotto tickets might be winners.

Late Sunday night there was a knock at the door. Lavigueur's 18-year-old son Yves answered, only to find a stranger yammering in English. "I threw him out," the French-speaking Yves told reporters. "The guy had $7 million to give me, and I told him to get out. It was ten-thirty at night, and I didn't understand a word he was saying. I thought he was a thief."

Fortunately for the Lavigueurs, Bill Murphy was persistent. He came back the following night with a bilingual friend, who announced to Jean-Guy, "You're a millionaire!"

Of course, Lavigueur could not believe his ears. But after taking one look at the ticket he realized that luck was finally on his side. He slapped Murphy on the back, promised him a $100,000 reward for returning the ticket, and cracked open a case of beer.

An hour and several Molson's later, the reward had doubled. And by the end of the night, Lavigueur had decided to give Murphy a cool million. After all, as Jean-Guy himself said that night, how many honest people are there around these days?

At an April Fools' Day press conference the next day, Jean-Guy Lavigueur announced that the money would be split equally six ways. Murphy would get his share, of course, as would the five members of the family lottery pool: Jean-Guy, his sons Yves and Michel, daughter Sylvie, and brother-in-law Jean-Marie Deaudelin. Lavigueur senior seemed to enjoy the spotlight. He answered all the reporters questions, made jokes about his fondness for Molson's beer, and even planted a big, wet kiss on Bill Murphy's cheek, just for the cameras.

The Lavigueurs' tale of lost and found luck was the kind of good news story that lottery officials dream about, and made the family instant celebrities. Every paper and news broadcast in Canada ran a story on these star-crossed winners; their pictures even graced the

---

LIKE FATHER, LIKE SON

On August 6, 1994, an amazing coincidence occurred: Edgar Sellwood and his son Mike, of Spruce Grove, Alberta, both won over $1 million on separate Lotto 6/49 tickets.

---

pages of *People* magazine.

But with fame came problems. The Lavigueurs were besieged with reporters, well-wishers, long-forgotten friends, and everyday joes who just wanted a handout. One ballsy taxi driver knocked on the door and asked for a couple thousand dollars to open up a donut shop.

Bill Murphy very quickly tired of the public glare. Soon after the story broke, he managed to slip back into oblivion, and has eluded reporters to this day.

The Lavigueurs were not so lucky. Within weeks of the win, the public relations dream turned into a pitchman's nightmare. Another Lavigueur came forward crying, and petitioned the Courts to freeze her family's new-found fortune. It was Louise, Jean-Guy's estranged daughter whom he kicked out of the house just before the Lotto draw because she'd missed a curfew. Louise, 16, didn't know anything about the big win until she phoned her dad on Tuesday night. In her statement to the Court, Louise said that her father's message was short and far from sweet.

"You are a damned fool," he told Louise. "It's your fault you weren't there. You have just lost $1.5 million. I have to go. I have other calls to make. Goodbye."

Louise figured it was just an early April Fools' joke, but the next day, when the story hit the papers, she wasn't laughing. Louise believed that her family had defrauded her out of her share of the jackpot. After all, she'd paid $2 into the family lottery fund every week since January. That she hadn't paid the week of the draw was a minor point: her father had barred her from the house, how could she pay? Besides, the family had extra money in the pool from the odd $10 win. The winning ticket could have easily been bought with some of that money.

To add insult to financial injury, Louise told the judge that her family didn't invite her along on their celebratory Guadeloupe holiday. Jean-Guy had a few more choice words for his daughter. "He told me to go out and buy a funeral notice, because as far as he was concerned, I was dead," Louise said in her statement.

The young outcast got the judge to freeze the family bank account.

KIDS WIN THE DARNDEST THINGS

 Next time you buy your kid a lottery ticket, remember the story of Walter Blomquist.

He didn't think twice when he asked his 12-year-old daughter Colleen to fill out an Irish Sweepstakes ticket.

"What name should I write in the little box, Daddy?"

"Any name you like. . . ."

That was back in February 1971.

This simple exchange came back to haunt Blomquist a little while later when a horse named Double Cream finished first in the Derby, and young Colleen was left holding a $143,000 winning ticket . . . in her own name. Things seemed fine at first. The family, who lived in a small town near Sicamous, Manitoba, apparently treated the lucky ticket as a gift to the girl.

But a rift soon appeared, and Dad wound up taking daughter to court. Walter claimed that since he bought the ticket, he was the rightful owner of the prize money. The judge disagreed, and awarded the money to Colleen, to be held in public trust until she turned 18. And this is not the only example of a parent's good intentions gone bad. Consider the case of Ronald MacSporran. In 1982, this St. Catherines, Ontario auto-worker bought some tickets on a Rotary Club Raffle while visiting Edmonton, Alberta during Klondike Days. He signed his own name on some of the tickets, and on others he put the names of his wife and daughters.

"If we were lucky enough to have the winning ticket, I considered the prize to be a family one shared by the four of us," Ron explained at the time. As it turns out, they did have the winning ticket, and drove away with first prize, a $53,000 motor home. The only problem was

The family countered with an offer to set up a $125,000 trust fund for Louise, which she promptly rejected. "I refused to be bought," she defiantly told a reporter from *The Montreal Gazette*.

By now, the family was front page news again, and while embarrassed lottery officials waited for the whole thing to blow over, the rest of the country wondered if there wasn't a lesson to be learned. Maybe some blessings were too good to be true?

that the ticket was in his five-year-old daughter's name.

Enter the Alberta public trustee, who told Ronald that the motor home legally belonged to his daughter, and he would have to sell it and put the money in a trust fund for her until she turned 19. Remember, the trustee was acting on its own accord; Ronald's daughter hadn't uttered a word of complaint about the motor home.

"I understand Mr. MacSporran filled out one ticket in the name of the family dog," an official from the Public Trustee's office said. "It's too bad the dog didn't win. There wouldn't be a problem."

Similarly, in 1994, two-year-old Kayla Chambers of Edmonton won an $80,000 Jaguar XJS convertible on a ticket bought by her grandfather. Again the Alberta government interceded, sold the car and put the money in a trust account. With an average annual return of 8 percent, little Kayla could afford a $300,000 party to celebrate her 18th birthday. Get the message?

Many jurisdictions don't allow underage children to buy lottery tickets, although someone of legal age can assign any name to a ticket. As generous as you are, it isn't a good idea to assign lottery or raffle tickets to your children, grandchildren, nieces or nephews. Any prize automatically becomes that child's legal property, and even as a parent, you have limited access to it. Even if your kid wants you to give it to you, they can't. In most states and provinces the money is held in a public trust account where it collects interest at the prime rate minus two percent. Technically, any amount your child wins on the lottery should be held in trust for them until they reach the age of majority, anywhere from 18 to 21. Only in rare cases, like medical emergencies, would you have access to money held in trust and even then it can difficult.

Here's our expert advice then: even if you plan to give your underage children some or all of your lottery bonanza, don't write their names on the tickets. Give them the money after you've won it, and that way you're able to maintain control over it.

July 26, 1986, and another Lavigueur press conference. It was a touching scene: Father and daughter kiss and make up as the cameras roll.

"I have learned the most important thing in life is the love of your parents," Louise Lavigueur explained to media. "It's much more important than money, which is why I want to drop all legal action against my family."

The reconciliation came after a negotiation session in a Laval hotel.

LIKE MOTHER, LIKE SON

 Phyllis Klingbiel and her son Michael had something in common, besides a wacky last name. Both of them claimed a share of a $2.17 million winning ticket.

It seems that for years the two had been chipping in $20 a month each to buy lottery tickets. When their numbers finally came up, though, Michael cashed the ticket himself. His story was that he'd bought the ticket separately from their regular pool. Mom disagreed, and took her son to court. Meanwhile, Anthony Boscia, the owner of the liquor store where the Klingbiels bought their winning ticket, had his own ideas about what to do with the $1,000 sellers bonus he received. "I'm taking my family out for a wonderful time," he told *Time* magazine, "and that includes my parents."

Apparently, a deal was struck: Louise would be welcomed back into the family fold, and in return she would drop her lawsuit. Not everyone was happy with the result. Louise's lawyer was out about $5,000 in legal fees; hired under legal aid, the lawyer could only collect if there was a judgment in the case. The girl's court-appointed guardian Guy Trudeau was also upset.

"I certainly don't agree her case should be dropped until we know the conditions of her return home," he said.

These days, the Lavigueurs don't talk to the press much. In fact, Jean-Guy's last public appearance was a televised interview he gave in November 1989. His lottery luck left him sounding somewhat bitter. Old friends and family had turned their backs on him, he said, because he didn't give them enough money.

"To make everybody happy, I would have to give away all my money until I had nothing left and was back on welfare," he complained.

After making peace with his daughter—although their relationship remained a rocky one—Lavigueur moved his family into an $850,000, 17-room mansion just outside of Laval. To this day, the curious drive to the gates of the Lavigueur compound to peer through the heavy fence and wonder at the luxurious life of this famous First Family of the luck of the draw.

Sometimes lottery feuds can get downright ugly. Take the case of Mary Ellen Futch of Riverview, Florida. In September of 1984, the 65 year-old won $5 million in Lotto 6/49.

Futch bought her dream home and went on a spending spree, buying gifts for friends and family. She tried her hand at investing, including a disastrous bid to start a campground in Ontario.

The one person she forgot to spend money on was Uncle Sam, and when the tax collector came knocking, things went from bad to unbelievable. Barely three years after her win, Futch traded in her dream mansion for a trailer home in the face of a $500,000 bill for back taxes and penalties.

But wait, there's more. In August 1984, she was arrested for allegedly conspiring to have her daughter-in-law murdered. The evidence against her seemed strong: she'd offered a cop, posing as a contract killer, $5,000 to do the dirty deed.

And you thought your mother-in-law was bad news.

Canada's very first Olympic Lottery, on April 15, 1974, led to a family feud that turned out to be a dilly, pitting a cost account supervisor against his elderly in-laws.

Newspapers across Canada carried the smiling face of Roy Brooks, a

---

RUNNING, AND HIDING, IN THE FAMILY

It's the lottery winner's worst fear: someone, some day, will come out of the shadows and threaten their family. While most lottery winners never have to deal with this possibility, some people find that it is part and parcel of the luck of the draw.

Take the case of a family living just outside of Edmonton, Alberta. A short time after winning a large lottery jackpot, one of the winners found a note in the mailbox. The writer demanded $1 million or else he would "return to kill half your family, and you." The family called the police, and went into hiding.

The police staged a phony drop-off and waited for their catch. Eventually, a man named Doug Kinsella drove past. A few hours later he returned, picked up the package, and drove away. Police pulled him over and arrested him for extortion. Later, Kinsella told the judge that he needed the money to open a nightclub. The judge—who probably wasn't a club-goer—sentenced Kinsella to two years in the slammer.

YOU CAN'T TAKE IT WITH YOU

 Here's a simple rule of thumb: if you win a lottery, or come into any sudden fortune, make a will. It will save surviving relatives and friends endless grief.

Solomon Keith of New York City was one winner who didn't write a will, which left his lotto legacy in limbo when he was killed in a car accident. After months of debate, Keith's benefactors finally came up with a unique solution. They agreed to auction off the remaining $3.8 million to the highest bidder; like most American jackpots, Keith's was being paid in annual installments, and he still had 16 years to go when he died. A life insurance company came up with the winning bid of $2,075,000—which was left to Keith's relatives to divvy up amongst themselves.

Keith's relatives got off easy when you consider the story of Johnny Rae Brewster. This Texas Lottery winner was a Dallas pharmacist who won almost $13 million in 1995; ten months later, he died of a heart attack, leaving everything to his sister, including a $3.5 million tax bill. Under Texas law, upon death the estate has to pay the entire tax owing, even though the yearly payouts amounted to just over $460,000. They then came up with a happy compromise. They'd let Brewster's sister pay the tax in installments over ten years, at a cost of $482,000 a year. Talk about your lucky break.

gentle-looking man who'd claimed the $500,000 second prize in the Olympic Lottery. Since the nine tobacco factory workers split the $1 million jackpot, Brooks was the biggest single winner—at a time when half a million dollars seemed like an absolute fortune.

"It will take a while to come down to earth," Brooks said in an interview. "It will be life as usual."

In fact, it only took Brooks a few days to come back to earth. That's when his in-laws, Fred and Nora Price, returned from a Florida vacation to demand their share of the windfall. The Prices claimed that they had a formal agreement to split the costs, and rewards, of the lottery ticket. The Brooks said that no such deal existed. Out of the goodness of their hearts, though, they offered his wife's parents $75,000, payable in installments to minimize the gift tax. But the Prices refused, and the fight dragged on for more than three years. Just before the trial began, the parties reached a settlement: Fred and Nora got $77,500 in addition to the $40,000 they'd already received. One can only imagine that things were a little strained at the next family reunion.

And then, there's the story of Hubert and Eric Lavoie, a father and son denied their share of a winning lottery ticket, and subsequently fired from their jobs by . . . Hubert's nephew, Michel Guay.

The three Quebecers worked together and had been sharing lottery tickets for three years before their number came up in June 1993.

The next morning, Hubert got a call from his nephew: don't bother coming in to work today, or for that matter, any day. When Eric showed up, he found the company doors locked and the building empty. Guay and his partner had gone off to collect their lottery winnings.

The matter went to court, where Guay claimed that his uncle and cousin had not paid their two dollars the week of the draw, and were therefore not entitled to share the winnings. The judge disagreed. He said that the Lavoies had been playing and paying long enough to prove their good faith. The judge ordered Guay to cough up $166,666.

While the Lavoies got their just reward, they remained jobless . . . although they probably saved a little money, with one less relative on their Christmas gift list.

Chapter 8

Friends

A winning lottery ticket can earn you fast friends, and even faster enemies. Just ask Frank Capaci, who's seen first hand the highs and lows of the luck of the draw—although, admittedly, his highs were higher than almost anyone else in history.

It all began back in May, 1998, during the first great Powerball feeding frenzies. The jackpot had rolled over several times and the prize pool was approaching $200 million. It was a record—albeit one that would fall in a few months. That's when John Marnell and Patti Rooney, a couple of the bartenders at Bill's on Bartlett's Pizza Pub in Streamwood, Illinois, decided to make the trek across the state line to a grocery store in Pell Lake, Wisconsin to pick up some tickets on the draw. They collected $180 from customers, including five dollars from Frank Capaci and his wife Shirley. Capaci, a retired electrician, was a regular in the bar, and often took part in the pools and other special events.

After buying the tickets, the bartenders put one in an envelope for everyone in the pool. Shortly after the draw, a wave of excitement ran through the bar: news reports were saying the winning ticket, worth a whopping $195 million, had been bought in Pell Lake. The Capacis didn't show up at the bar until the afternoon after the draw. People joked with Frank as he opened his envelope, but when they saw his face, they knew something was up. He looked stunned, and didn't utter a single word. After the shock had worn off, Capaci reportedly dashed off $10,000 checks to Rooney and Marnell, the bartenders, apparently promising them more once he'd collected the jackpot.

The next day Frank and his wife showed up at the lottery office to claim their prize. They seemed a publicist's dream come true: Frank in his blue golf shirt, Shirley in her red windbreaker, talking about sharing their fortune with family and friends.

"I don't want a Porsche or anything like that," Capaci told the assembled reporters. "I want a motorcycle: a Harley. I'm going to take my wife on a tour of the U.S."

The next day, Frank showed up for his part-time job, mowing lawns at the Poplar Creek Country Club in nearby Huffman Estates. He joked that he didn't want to lose his job. But over the ensuing weeks and months, the lustre began to wear off Capaci's win. In April 1999, *Newsweek* reported that many of Capaci's closest friends no longer talked to him. He was no longer welcome at his neighborhood pub, where early offers to share the wealth had not been followed through. There were rumblings that the bartenders were considering a lawsuit. And although he still worked mowing lawns, he had an unlisted phone number and, by the sounds of things, was in the market for a whole new crop of friends.

It's a common story: lucky lottery winners who find old friends fading fast. It could be a matter of simple jealousy, or it could be that, despite winners' claims to the contrary, money does change them. Of course, it's not always the case, particularly where lower level jackpots are concerned. In fact, it's possible for people to win the lottery—even share a lottery win with a friend—without finding themselves on the outside looking in. Dave Egner of Regina, Saskatchewan, is living proof. In his lifetime he's won all sorts of things, from a year's supply of beer to an all-expense paid trip for two to Australia. And in May 1983, while he was the financially secure co-owner of a successful body shop, Dave shared a million dollar lottery jackpot with a friend.

"I think luck is something that people create for themselves, through perseverance. I know that luck can come about, but a person earnestly has to try to make it work, to make it happen. How many times have you seen that slogan, the harder I try the luckier I get?"

Dave won the jackpot on the Super Lotto, with his ticket partner and co-worker Kay Hahn. Although not as popular as group play, a lot of lottery players enjoy sharing a ticket with a friend. Dave says that the ticket partnership allowed him to spend a little more time with Kay during the week; it also had some practical advantages.

"I used to dread coughing up ten bucks every week. I'd say to myself, Oh god, here we go again! I'd tried to stay out of the whole process as much as possible. I told Kay that I didn't want to keep the tickets. I would

HOWDY, PARTNER

The strangest ticket partnership on record belongs to John Inglis and Robert Alexander, two seamen who shared a $1 million Lotto Canada jackpot in the summer of 1978.

John was a baker aboard the *Pinebog*, a government ship that brought supplies to military stations in Canada's Arctic. One morning, he woke up with an unlucky feeling. As he later told a reporter, he tried to sell his lottery ticket.

"I was playing bridge in the mess hall and asked about ten people if they'd buy half of it. But they had a pool of ten tickets already, so nobody wanted it."

Finally, Bob coughed up five bucks.

Not much of a story so far, but what you have to realize is that the draw was held 18 hours before John sold half his ticket. The radio reception was poor on the *Pinebog*, and John certainly wasn't about to check for winning numbers in the morning paper, so he had no idea that the ticket he held was worth a million bucks.

"I'm not mad or bitter or anything," John said at his press conference. "I'm happy I won half of it. We probably won because of our combined luck."

buy one from her, but I just asked her to keep it for me. If I won, fine; if I didn't, fine."

One Monday morning when he showed up for work, Dave thanked his lucky stars for a dedicated friend like Kay. "Kay came up to me and said that she had something she wanted to tell me. And I didn't know what the hell it was. And when she said that we'd won a million, I'll tell you, my blood pressure rose like you wouldn't believe; my heart started pounding. I was just in shock. I couldn't believe it."

How did Dave react to his half-million dollar windfall? Well, he didn't run out and quit his job, but in retrospect, he believes that maybe he should have. "The win sort of threw me off. It happened at a time I least expected it. The biggest mistake I made was that I should have left the body shop as soon as I got the money. What happened was, the salary I was making from the autobody repair business, plus I invested all the prize money at Canada Trust so I was making income from that—the taxes I had to pay! It really wasn't worth it. I would have been better off to sell out of my business and do what I wanted to do."

Dave isn't looking for sympathy. He says that winning the lottery was a great experience. But at the time, he was already a successful business-man. He owned half of Regina Auto Body, the company he'd taken over from his father in 1964. The company had thrived and by 1983, on paper at least, Dave was already a millionaire. After the Super Lotto win he could have sold his shares and, with a little prudence, lived comfortably for the rest of his life. But he stayed on the job for seven more years. How come?

At first, he says, he was being something of a martyr, going to work to show that the lottery win hadn't changed him. But more importantly, he loved his job and the people he worked with; it gave him something meaningful to do everyday. There were also the financial considerations. While most of us dream of winning big on the lottery someday, we never really consider how far the money will go. After you pay off your mort-gage and other debts, buy a new car, go on a trip, and maybe give a little to family and friends—well, half a million dollars can dwindle away pret-ty fast if you're not careful.

"A lot of people say, you've really got it made, you've got a lot of money. Actually, you don't have a lot of money because you have to man-age it the same way you managed money before you won. If you don't, you'll end up with nothing. When you're working, you've got a source of income that's revolving; it just keeps coming in. Investment income is much more vulnerable: interest rates fluctuate, stocks go up and down. There are a lot of variables."

In other words, Dave views his windfall the same way he views his lifelong string of good luck: you can't just leave things to blind chance. For her part, Kay had little to say about her half of the win. She declined to be interviewed for this book, but did say that part of what made the win so special was that she got to share it with a friend. Dave agrees.

"It's one thing to win a lottery jackpot on your own, I think. But when you win it with someone you know, it just makes it all the more better. It's like anything else; it's more fun if you do it with people you care about."

Dave is now in his late 50s and semi-retired. He spends his time work-ing around the house, helping out at a local church, skiing and golfing. And by the way, he still plays the lottery.

"Lotteries really are the best thing. The reason why they are the best is because a person is only investing five dollars, ten dollars, twenty dol-lars—whatever the case may be. But then that's it. They have to wait for the draw. But now we're getting into other kinds of gambling with casinos and video slot machines, and I think we're getting into a bad situation. You can go into a casino and spend $40 or $50, or $100, and you may lose all of it."

LOTTERY PARTNERSHIP AGREEMENT

When you share a lottery ticket with a friend, particularly if you're buying tickets with any regularity, you've effectively entered into a legal partnership. It's a good idea, a very good idea, to put things down in writing so they don't come back to haunt you.

LOTTERY TICKET PARTNERSHIP AGREEMENT

Agreement between   and   and   .

The above parties agree to share the costs and benefits of lottery tickets purchased only for the lottery games and draws specified below. Each party owns an equal share, unless otherwise specified in writing.

In the event of the death of either party, any pending or outstanding benefits will go to that partner's estate.

This agreement can be terminated at any time by either partner with written notification. Termination does not affect the outcome of tickets prior to notification.

LOTTERY TICKET PARTNERSHIP AGREEMENT FORM

GAME NAME	DRAW DAYS	DURATION OF AGREEMENT
1.		
2.		
3.		
4.		
5.		

It might sound strange that a man who has played lotteries all his life, and who enjoys the odd trip to Las Vegas, would be opposed to some of the new directions provincial lottery corporations are heading, but he has a personal interest. His wife is a clinical psychologist who works for the Saskatchewan government and is helping to develop strategies to deal with people who become addicted to video lottery games. Dave has some advice for people who want to share in his good fortune. The most important element of luck, he says, is risk.

"Accept the danger in risk. That, I think, plays a big part in luck. If you're not willing to accept risk, you're not going to be lucky at all, you're not opening the doors for luck."

FREE SUBSCRIPTION ADVICE

Playing partners? Why don't you go for a ticket subscription option. Since the lottery people insist that all tickets partners be listed on the subscription form, there will be a record of your agreement and less chance for arguments when the money starts rolling in.

Dave Egner was doubly lucky. Not only did he win a million, but he kept his friendship with co-winner Kay Hahn intact. That isn't always the case. Often, the promise of big bucks turns the best of friends into sworn enemies.

The case of Manitoba's millionaire house painter is typical. In October 1990, Giovanni and Maria Garofalo of Winnipeg claimed a $2.6 million Lotto 6/49 jackpot, the fifth highest prize awarded in that province up to that time.

Almost immediately, John Costantinidis called foul. Costantinidis was friends with the Garofalo's son, a painter named Rocco, and claimed that the younger Garofalo was the real lottery winner. Rocco had his parents claim the prize, Costantinidis alleged, to get out of paying his friend a share of the jackpot. John went on to say that he and Rocco had an unwritten agreement to buy 6/49 tickets and split any winnings. For their part, the Garofalos denied any improprieties, and the case was left for the courts to decide.

One of the strangest stories of friendship-gone-bad revolves around a piece of five-dollar plumbing pipe. The tale took place ten years ago in Port Hardy, on the northern tip of Vancouver Island. Eduardo Quiamco was helping add an extension onto his friend Ruffino Gaspar's mobile home when they realized they needed a small piece of pipe to finish the job. Eduardo went out and bought the pipe, and in return Ruffino offered to split his ten-dollar Super Lotto ticket.

The ticket turned out to be a $1 million winner, a little detail that Ruffino neglected to share with his helpful friend. When Eduardo finally got wind of the windfall, he took Ruffino to court, claiming half of the prize. The judge ruled in Eduardo's favor. On the bright side, Ruffino could now brag that he'd put a half-million-dollar extension on his mobile home.

What do Coca-Cola, Kentucky Fried Chicken, and your favorite set of lottery numbers have in common? Well, in the eyes of at least one Victoria, B.C. lawyer, they are all secret formulas entitled to special protection under the law.

In the summer of 1987, Helen Campbell took Wilma Crothers to court, claiming that she deserved half of her (former) friend's $1.6 million jackpot. Neither party disputed the basic facts of the case: several months earlier, they'd agreed to two sets of numbers to play in Lotto 6/49. However, Wilma said the agreement counted for Saturday draws only, and since she won on a Wednesday, she didn't owe her friend a thing. Helen maintained that there was no "Saturdays only" rule.

Here's where things got interesting. Helen's lawyer, David Wilson, argued that the two women had essentially formed a legal partnership whose sole purpose was to enter two specific sets of numbers into the Lotto 6/49 draw. Wilson said that these numbers, which Wilma had also used in her Wednesday night win, constituted a "formula capable of getting into the coffers of Lotto 6/49—a formula for winning and a formula that can be protected under law."

In other words, it didn't matter which day of the week the draw was held: the numbers belonged to both women.

Unfortunately, the judge never got to rule on this curious question. Minutes before the court was to make a decision, Wilma's husband flipped a dime: heads, they leave the fate in the hands of the judge; tails, they settle out of court. Tails it was, and Helen was awarded a sizable settlement. No word, though, on who got custody of the numbers. . . .

Some people will go to any extreme to hoard their lottery treasure, but few have gone as far as Serafin Guerra. In March 1982, this Kitimat, B.C., man won $1 million on Super Lotto. But then he found himself embroiled in a battle with a family friend, Laurinda Gonclaves, who claimed that the two of them regularly bought lottery tickets together and had agreed to share any winnings.

The case went to court, and a judge ordered Serafin to set aside $442,000 in an interest-bearing account until the dispute was settled. But before the judge heard the case, Serafin, literally, took the money and ran . . . back to his homeland, Portugal.

In Serafin's absence, Gonclaves, a widowed mother of four, was awarded half the jackpot. As for collecting the money, that was another story. As far as we know, Gonclaves is still waiting.

There he was, calm, cool, collected, smiling for the cameras.

"I'm not going to change or let this run away with me," James

A POPULAR GUY

With friends like Leonard Sanders Sr., people don't need . . . more friends. After winning $20 million in the Illinois lottery, Sanders set off to share the money with everyone in his town. One of the first things he did was to buy an empty building and convert it into a seniors' center, and chipped in $100,000 to restore a century-old Baptist church.

Sanders, a retired coal miner who had been playing the lottery for 25 years before he hit it big in 1996, took his philanthropy in stride. "I just did what I thought I had to do," Sanders told *Jet* magazine. "I really don't want a whole lot of praise for it."

Nicholas told reporters who asked him about the almost $1.3 million Lottario win in April 1979.

The jackpot was huge for its day; the pool had grown for more than two months, and it took Nicholas another month to step forward and claim his prize. He told the *Globe & Mail* that he'd needed the time to let the excitement fade and clear his head. In the eyes of the Ontario Lottery Corporation, he must have seemed the perfect winner for such a high profile prize.

But the story soon turned in to the kind of PR nightmare that lottery officials dread. The ticket was actually bought by a Dr. Mergeri Ede, a Nigerian immigrant living in Kingston, Ontario. When Dr. Ede realized he had the winning ticket, he wanted to avoid all the publicity, so he passed it on to his friend James Nicholas who, in return for a few thousand dollars, was to claim the ticket for Ede.

The case very quickly made its way to court, with everyone—including a shadowy charitable foundation that both men were associated with—suing everyone else. The battling parties couldn't even agree where to keep the money in trust while the legal arguments dragged on. Last we heard, the former friends were still fighting it out, proving that a friend in need is a friend indeed.

Especially if he has a winning lottery ticket.

CHAPTER 9

LOVE AND SEX

They say love conquers all, but can love endure the pressure of a multi-million dollar jackpot win?

Paul and Danielle LeBlanc (not their real names) are one couple who put their love, and a 30-year marriage, to the lottery test. In the spring of 1994, Paul bought a quick pick on Lotto 6/49, 45 minutes before the terminals closed. Next morning, he took the ticket with him to work—a car wash he and his wife owned north of Edmonton. As he checked the lottery numbers in the paper, he realized that he was holding a winning ticket.

"My legs became weak and my heart started pounding because it's hard to believe. A lot of things go through your mind. You don't want to get too high. I mean, what if the numbers are wrong? When the numbers are printed in the paper, there is always the possibility of a mistake. I didn't want to get too excited."

Paul called the store where he'd bought the ticket, to double check his number. The clerk confirmed the win.

"Then I got really excited, and I forgot to ask how much I had won. About a half an hour after we settled down, we called again and they told us that there were two winners, and that I had won $1.2 million. It's still hard to believe."

Paul was a veteran 6/49 player who'd been buying tickets ever since the draw started. Danielle, on the other hand, rarely bought lottery tickets of any kind, and when she did it was usually as a birthday or Christmas gift for Paul. But that morning, when he called to tell her that they'd just won "the Big One," she knew exactly what he was talking about. When it came to convincing the rest of their family, though, Paul had a hard time.

"I'm the type of guy who always jokes around, and my kids didn't want to believe me. They said things like, 'Don't say things like this when you know it isn't true.' Everybody that we called acted like that. So Danielle finally had to get on the line and tell them, and they believed her, because she's the type of person who would never joke about a thing like that."

With the winning ticket firmly in their hands, Paul and Danielle took some time to get their affairs in order. They needed a day just to recover from the shock, and then they talked to their lawyer, accountant, and financial adviser. But business wasn't the only thing on their minds. As Danielle explains, they had personal concerns as well.

"The thing that sticks in my mind is my privacy. Like when I went shopping, I didn't want people gawking at me. And we have a grandchild, and I became very over-protective; I didn't want even the fact mentioned. I was afraid that there was somebody out there who would kidnap the child and say they'd want a million bucks. We were scared what was going to happen to us—the phone, the door, people bombarding us. But nothing ever happened."

Finally, five days after their win, Paul and Danielle drove to the Western Canada Lottery office in Edmonton to collect their winnings. But they still hadn't got used to their new-found "millionaire" status.

"The girl from the lottery asked us if we stayed in the President's Suite at the hotel," Danielle recalls. "We hadn't even thought about it. We just took an ordinary room. Nothing like that occurred to us. We're just common people, we've always looked after our money. We didn't spend foolishly. Even now today, when we look at something, we just don't buy it. We shop around. The old ways are still there."

Old habits may die hard, but that doesn't mean the LeBlancs aren't learning to enjoy their windfall. They've sold their business and now enjoy "semi-retirement," although they're still only in their early 50s.

"One million is just enough to retire comfortably," Paul says. "We have enough to do the little bit of travelling we want to do, and help our kids. But, the money has got to last us the rest of our lives. We can't go overboard. We like to keep living our lifestyle. It's a decent lifestyle but not extravagant."

Has winning the lottery changed their relationship? Paul says that most of the after-effects have been positive. "We have more time to spend together doing the things we've always wanted to do. And we don't have to worry so much about money. Sure, we have to watch ourselves, but we

Your Money or Your Wife (or Husband)

So that no-good, stinking, dirty excuse-for-a-man you married just won a million bucks, and you figure that now's your chance to take your share of the money and run. You may want to think twice before you leave him, because you might not get half of his jackpot. Our experts tell us that lottery winnings are not specifically covered in any existing divorce laws, and individual cases would be treated quite differently from state to state or province to province.

One important question is, how did your spouse get the ticket in the first place? If it was a gift, then it's unlikely that you would have any claim over the subsequent winnings, unless the money was used to buy something clearly intended as a joint family asset (a house or gerbil, for example). In those cases, you may have a claim on the assets.

If your spouse bought the ticket or somehow won it, then you probably have some kind of claim over any leftover money, or stuff bought with the jackpot—again, depending on where you live. If your spouse won the money before you were married, don't expect to get your hands on any of it; the law says that anything you bring with you to a marriage, you can take with you when you leave. Still, if your ex is earning income from lottery winnings, the judge will probably take that into account when it comes to alimony and child support.

don't have to lie awake at night worrying about how we're going to pay our bills."

Still, Danielle sees how such a sudden windfall could strain some relationships.

"There could be problems if the couple didn't agree on what to do with the money. Ours wasn't a whole lot of money. We both knew that we just couldn't spend it; we knew that we had to invest wisely. And that we could only use so much a year. We were both in agreement. But if we weren't in agreement—I don't know. . . ."

A lottery win doesn't always mean a life of bliss for couples.

Just ask Doreen Holgate. After winning a million in 1977 on the Western Express, her fiancé Wilfred Stoeser called off the wedding, then sued her for half the jackpot. Likewise, Lady Luck was the "other woman" in Althea Millin's love life. On August 10, 1988, this Richmond, B.C., woman

TOP TEN SIGNS YOU'RE PAYING TOO MUCH ATTENTION TO THE LOTTERY, AND NOT ENOUGH ATTENTION TO YOUR SPOUSE

10. During the height of passion, you scream out your favorite 6/49 numbers.
9. You just don't scratch his cards the way you used to.
8. Powerball has taken on a whole new meaning for you.
7. Your idea of foreplay is Pick-3 plus a bonus number.
6. Your last conversation at the breakfast table went like this: "Hey stupid, read me the winning numbers."
5. Every time you try to get romantic, she says, "Not tonight, I have a bonus draw."
4. You find yourself deliberately missing a few draws in the hopes his jackpot gets bigger.
3. To enhance lovemaking, you force your spouse to dress up like a convenience store clerk.
2. You stumble into the house late at night, stinking of cheap liquor, and mumbling the phrase "quick pick" over and over again.
1. Last night you got real confused, and tried to scrape off his under wear with a quarter.

got a phone call from fiancé Owen Edmonds. He wanted to tell her that he'd collected half a million dollars on Lotto 6/49. But he had other news.

"He had the cheek to call me collect, tell me about all this money he'd just won, and then say we weren't getting married," Althea complained to the papers.

"I was wearing his ring. I thought we were making plans."

Then there's the case of Sharif Ali. The Toronto Star reported that in August 1981, Ali won close to $600,000 on Lottario. Strangely, though, after finding out he had the winning ticket, he waited until the next morning to quietly break the news to his wife and children.

A few days later it became clear why Ali wasn't exactly jumping for joy over the win when Milica Skarec, a co-worker, confronted him and demanded her share of the jackpot. This wasn't your typical office pool— Ali and Skarec were secret lovers who'd also shared a passion for buying lottery tickets.

Ali refused to give Skarec any money, and denied having an affair

---

IT DIDN'T HAPPEN TO ME

In the 1994 movie *It Could Happen to You,* Nicolas Cage plays a cop who gives half his million dollar lottery jackpot to waitress Bridget Fonda. In the movie, Cage winds up leaving his scheming wife in favor of the upfront and honest Fonda. But Robert Cunningham—whose real life story inspired the film—told *People* magazine that in this case, life didn't really imitate art.

Rather than pay a tip, Cunningham asked waitress Phyllis Penzo if she wanted to share a lottery ticket with him. Together, they selected six numbers. A little while later, they hit a $6 million payday. Cunningham amicably split the winnings with Penzo, and neither winner ever left their spouse. "We were just friends," Penzo said of her relationship with her co-winner.

Of course, "just friends" isn't big box office.

---

with her. But a judge saw things differently, and awarded Skarec her half, plus interest.

In another celebrated case, a Welland, Ontario, tow truck driver took his lottery windfall and hauled his butt out of town, leaving behind his wife of 19 years.

"I was sitting in front of the next-door neighbor's house talking for most of the evening and when I came in he was gone," Joan Meehan explained to the press after her husband Robert skipped town. "He didn't even leave a note."

In fact, he didn't even tell his wife that he'd won $100,000 in the lottery. She found out about it when a reporter called to interview wayward Bob about his good fortune.

"He left me with $6 in my wallet and $11 in my bank account," Joan complained. "Now I have nothing except bills."

But wait. Lotteries aren't always shameless home-wreckers. In at least one case, a lottery windfall played Cupid. On Christmas Day 1974, Annette Gagnon of Fauquier, Quebec was separated from her husband and on welfare. Her future seemed bleak.

But a few weeks later, her whole world changed when she won $330,000 in the Olympic Lottery. The money allowed her to buy the house of her dreams and a sky blue Lincoln Continental, and to indulge

THE WINNING BACHELOR

Brian Major wishes he kept his big mouth shut.

On the day he won $1.8 million in the Washington State Lottery, he quipped to the press, "Be sure to say that I'm single."

They did, and the 27-year-old millionaire faced a deluge of phone calls from prospective Mrs. Majors.

"Everybody wants to meet somebody, but I'm not in a hurry until I get everything straight," Major explained, adding that he'd stopped answering the phone. "I want to go back to being myself: plain, dull Brian."

her passion for bingo.

Annette's luck of the draw also helped her greatest wish come true; after three years apart, she and her husband reconciled. They say that the course of true love never runs smooth, and in Annette's case, apparently, it took a few hundred thousand dollars to calm the waters.

Oh, what a tangled web. . . .

The trouble started for Mohamed Helmy back in March 1991, when he sent his brother Andrew to the lottery office in Toronto to collect his $2.5 million Lotto 6/49 jackpot. Mohamed's marriage was on the rocks, and he hoped that this small deception would help him navigate Ontario's tricky divorce laws without having to shell out to his soon-to-be ex-wife.

"Mohamed came home all excited that his brother had won this lottery," Rose Helmy later told a reporter. "But it just seemed really strange, because it was Mohamed who was always playing the lottery."

Things got even stranger when, a little while later, Mohamed paid the remaining $100,000 on the family home, claiming that his brother had given him the money.

The web of deceit completely unraveled, though, when Mohamed opened a $700,000 trust account under his sister's name, with the understanding that she would not withdraw any money without his permission. In return, Mohamed says, he gave his sister and her husband the mortgage on a house. However, Mohamed's sister Foutna asserted that she and her brother had bought the ticket jointly, so half the money belonged to her.

The siblings wound up battling each other in court, with Mohamed enlisting the support of his ex-wife to try to prove that he was indeed the sole ticket buyer. In the meantime, Mohamed got a job with a glass-mak-

BIGGER THAN THE BOTH OF YOU

When Herman Fischer won $1 million in the Provincial Lottery ten years ago, his girlfriend was not happy.

"Why him?" Debbie Leitch lamented to the press. "Anything but a million. I'd preferred that it be $250,000 instead."

Her concern? Debbie contended that a man with money starts to act a little strange. "I'm sure it's going to change him in some way. No man can walk around with a million in his back pocket and stay the same."

For his part, the Edmonton telephone company administrator admitted that things would change, but promised to try to keep his head. Herman planned to spend more time taking it easy: hiking, playing tennis, and shooting basketball with friends. "That's what I'll probably spend my time doing. I don't go for smart dress and discotheques and fancy spots, though. They're too pretentious."

ing company and claimed that he lost an as yet unaccounted for million-dollar chunk of his money on a bad investment.

His ex thinks the cash has made its way to Egypt, but she suspects that no one will ever untangle the web of deceit.

You can run, but you can't hide. That's what John Gonslaves found out when the wife he abandoned 48 years earlier sued for retroactive child support and alimony. Marie Hynes was inspired to launch her lawsuit after seeing Gonslaves' smiling face in the paper; he'd just won $5.1 million in the Massachusetts Lottery. "He left me to suffer a lot," Hynes told reporters. "I felt like I deserve this for all this suffering."

CHAPTER 10

SUPERNATURAL

Are you interested in winning the lottery? Well, don't just dream about it. . . .

On second thought, do just dream about it. It's a surprisingly effective way to win. That's what Calgary's Terry Johnston suggests. Although Johnston has never won a major lottery jackpot, he has an interesting story to tell about the power of the subconscious mind. Call it ESP, the supernatural, or just plain strange. . . .

The story starts off when I accidentally phoned Johnston, 40, who shares the same name with a fellow Calgarian, who did win a million on the lottery a few years ago. In fact, as I was dialing his number I was thinking about how funny it would be if I got the wrong person, but he turned out to have a strange lottery story himself. The next thing I knew, Johnston answered the phone, and within moments had launched into his tale.

"I was working in radio in Port Alberni, B.C. I was making like $1,127 a month, and I just wasn't making ends meet. It was the baloney-sand-wich-in-the-hotel-room kind of thing. I got hold of a book from the library. It was about dreams and how you can jump ahead in time, pre-cognition, and visualize events in the future."

Johnston was particularly interested in the section about lotteries. As hokey as it sounded, he decided to give it a try.

"The main idea is that you tell yourself that you're not trying to think ahead in time, you're trying to think back. You've got your mind set to think, 'What were those numbers?' rather than, 'What will those numbers be?'"

That night, Johnston went to bed prepared to visualize his lottery win. But nothing happened. The next afternoon, he had a snooze before going in to do his evening shift at the radio station.

"I had this vivid dream. I met this little man, and he starts telling me these numbers. At any rate I woke up, and I could only remember four of the numbers. I wrote them down. Then I went in to work, and that night over the wire the lottery numbers came through. The first four were the same numbers that I'd written down. And the other two? As soon as I saw them I recognized them from my dream."

As a record, Johnston still has a photocopy of his ticket. The numbers he'd dreamt were 11, 15, 21, and 26; he also picked 31 and 36. The winning numbers for the next draw on February 26, 1986: 11, 15, 26, 33, 40, and 49.

The next week, Johnston tried again. This time, he remembered four numbers—7, 17, 28, 37—all of which came up on the March 8 Lotto 6/49 draw. Johnston was $86.50 richer.

With enough spending money to last a few weeks, Johnston was content. He stopped trying to remember his dreams, and soon forgot exactly how he did it.

"I've never been able to reproduce these dreams since then. I wish I could get hold of that book. Besides, money's not that big a deal to me. At the time it was just a matter of if I could get some groceries I'd be happy."

So some stranger on the phone claims to have won eighty bucks and change by listening to his dreams. Big deal! It's just a load of hogwash. Right?

Well, Terry Johnston doesn't think it's hogwash. And neither does Muriel Ecker. Late in 1993, Ecker had her own close encounter with the strange world of dreams.

"Either the day after or the day before Christmas, my son whowas living in Vancouver, phoned me up in the afternoon and said, 'You know, I had a dream last night. I can see those lotto numbers just as clear as can be, even still.'"

Son Wyeth Ecker passed on his dream numbers to his mother: 1, 3, 7, 8, 35, 44. "The only one he wasn't sure of was forty-four," Muriel Ecker recalls. "The forty-three seemed to be coming up quite a bit, so I said maybe I should play that number, too."

Muriel decided to give her son's dream numbers a try. The next month, she played his six numbers, plus another group of six replacing the 44 with a 43.

MIND OVER MATTERS

What would you do if you'd misplaced a $10.4 million winning lottery ticket?

That's the dilemma Paul Rousseau faced. His solution? He turned to the powers of the unconscious mind to try to find his missing treasure. It was June 1986 and Rousseau was traveling through Killam, a small town north of Edmonton, Alberta, when he pulled into the Town and Country Drug Mart. He bought a few things, including a ticket on the upcoming Lotto 6/49 draw. He put the ticket away, then promptly forgot about it.

Until two weeks later. That's when lottery officials appealed to the winner of the July 2 draw to step forward. The winning ticket, they said, was purchased in Killam. That's when the absent-minded Rousseau, a prospector from Edmonton, got a little edgy. He was sure his ticket was the winner, and even enlisted the help of a hypnotist and a clairvoyant to help him remember where he left the ticket.

Under hypnosis, Rousseau recalled that he was wearing a denim vest when he bought the ticket, and that he wore the same vest to the race track the next day. He also remembered that he'd picked up a hitchhiker, a young man from the U.S. who'd accidentally walked off with Rousseau's raincoat. Could the winning ticket be in the coat pocket? Or was it lying in a pile of litter somewhere at the race track?

Fortunately, the ticket turned up a few days later. Unfortunately for Rousseau, it turned up in the hands of Val and Ron Taylor, two hospital technicians from Killam who bought the ticket fair and square.

She kept playing and losing, but had a strong feeling for these numbers.

"Somebody asked me afterwards why I kept playing. Well, it only cost me a couple of dollars, and the thing that I kept remembering was how clear the numbers were in Wyeth's mind a few hours after he woke."

On January 29, just over a month after the initial conversation with her son, Muriel went through her post-Lotto draw routine. That night, as always, she phoned the lottery telephone line listed in the papers.

By the next morning, she says, she'd doubled-checked the numbers in five different places. No, she wasn't dreaming; she did have the winning ticket. She found herself almost one million dollars richer.

"I didn't find it nearly so strange as my son did. It was very funny. I

ALL I HAVE TO DO IS DIAL

Jo Jo is, apparently, a famous psychic who, definitely, runs a Psychic Hot Line, as advertised on her late night infomercial. She specializes in picking winning lottery numbers. Short on cash, Chris decided to give Jo Jo a try. It cost $4.99 per minute, pauses included.

JO JO: Hi, I'm Jo Jo. Thank you very much for calling my Psychic Alliance —

CHRIS: Hi, Jo Jo, this is Chris and —

JO JO:—My gifted psychics are available to help you 24 hours a day, seven days a week. Smile! Life is beautiful! Love you and kiss you! Please stay on the line. ...

ANNOUNCER: If you are calling from a touch tone phone, press "1" now.

CHRIS PRESSES 1.

ANNOUNCER: If you know the extension number of the psychic you'd like to speak with, press 1 now. If you would like to be connected to the next available psychic, press 2 now.

CHRIS PRESSES 2.

ANNOUNCER: Please hold while we connect your call.

10 SECOND PAUSE.

PSYCHIC: Hello.

CHRIS: Hi!

PSYCHIC: Welcome to the Psychic Line.

CHRIS: Hi, my name's Chris.

PSYCHIC: Sorry?

CHRIS: My name's Chris.

PSYCHIC: Chris. Okay. My name's Walter.

CHRIS: (aside)—a psychic named Walter?

(out loud) Hi, Walter!

PSYCHIC: And I read Tarot Cards.

CHRIS: Oh, you do?

PSYCHIC: Umm-hmm. And what is your date of birth?

CHRIS: September 3rd, 1959.

PSYCHIC: Okay. . . .

CHRIS: But I'll tell you what I'm really interested in. I'm going to buy a ticket on the Canadian lottery on Saturday, and I want to know what numbers would be good for me.

PSYCHIC: Okay. Just give me a second here. . . .

CHRIS: Are you dealing cards right now?

PSYCHIC: Right.

CHRIS: Whoa!
PSYCHIC: Just a moment. . . .
15 SECOND PAUSE.
PSYCHIC: First number is 14 . . . 17. . . 26 . . .
15 SECOND PAUSE.
PSYCHIC: Another second here. 37. . . 11. . .
23 SECOND PAUSE.
PSYCHIC: 34. And play Saturday. And you should play for the next four months as well.
CHRIS: Oh, really? With those numbers?
PSYCHIC: With those numbers.
CHRIS: Do you have a lot of people asking for lottery numbers?
PSYCHIC: Yeah.
CHRIS: Oh, really? I'd thought I'd be the only one.
PSYCHIC: No, you get a lot of people. That's why I don't say, you know, just yet, definitely for Saturday. If I could do that, you know, I wouldn't be doing this.
THEY LAUGH.
CHRIS: Well, do you do it for yourself then? Do you pick your lottery numbers by —
PSYCHIC:—Oh. I don't play the lottery. I probably should.
THEY LAUGH.
PSYCHIC: I don't do it, so, you know, when I do come up with numbers I forget to play it.
CHRIS: How come you don't play?
PSYCHIC: It just never crosses my mind. . . .
CHRIS: (aside) Wow, he must have a hectic schedule. . . .

* * *

Post script: Chris bought a lottery ticket with the lucky numbers that very day. He did not win on the draw the following Saturday, and three and a half months later, he's still waiting.

was very calm, cool, and collected. My family was quite a bit more excited. But even now, I sometimes have this feeling come over me—it's just incredible odds for something like that to happen that I'm kind of awed by it."

Has anyone been skeptical? There's been the odd comment behind her back, but she doesn't let it bother her. What has amazed her, though, is how far this story has spread. It even got a write-up in the tabloid the *National Examiner.*

"It was very accurate. There was only one thing wrong. They said that it was the last time I intended to play those numbers. I guess that was for dramatic effect, because I would have probably still been playing those numbers today if I hadn't won when I did."

If it sounds like she's taking it all in stride, maybe it's because she shares a trait common to winners.

"I always believed that I would win; I never doubted it. That fall before I won, my belief that I was going to win was very strong. I mentioned this to an acquaintance of mine. She was a little bit psychic, and she said, well, Muriel, do you know what the odds are for that? And I said, yes. And I also know that every time somebody wins, they've beaten those odds."

Still not convinced of the power of dreams? What if we throw a real live wolfman into the mix? A few years back, Jason Sanderson—known professionally as The Wolfman—was just another young guy trying to fulfill his dream of becoming a professional wrestler. He spent his days practicing choke holds and pile drivers, and his weekends in community halls and tiny arenas, plying his trade in and around his New Hampshire home.

While Jason was chasing his dream, his wife Mary was having dreams of her own. One vivid dream stood out, involving six numbers: 3, 5, 13, 18, 20, and 45. Mary asked her husband if she should play those numbers on an upcoming Powerball draw with a $66.4 million jackpot. Why not?

The next day, Mary went to the N-N Express convenience store and put her dollar down on a single ticket. A few hours later, the numbers were drawn. In an instant, thanks to his wife, The Wolfman transformed into the Richest Wrestler in the World.

Victor Bragg and his family needed a miracle.

In March 1978, the Victoria, B.C. electrician was driving home when he suffered a mild stroke. He spent that night in the hospital, where doctors seemed to have everything under control. But the next day, Bragg had a serious stroke—and eventually underwent a seven-and-a-half hour operation.

He was in hospital for over seven months, and by the time he was released his family was nearly broke. The father of five decided to sell their home of 18 years to make ends meet.

As a last-ditch effort, the family bought a ticket on the Western Express. Late in October, just as the family had given up hope, their

SWEET DREAMS

From vague notes and distant memories, Terry Johnston tried to piece together his lottery winning formula. Here are the six steps to sweet, and profitable, dreams.

Before you go to sleep you should:

1. Not try to look into the future; act as if the lottery has already taken place, and you are only trying to remember numbers already drawn.
2. Imagine the specific date and draw of your lotto win.
3. Tell yourself that you want to remember six numbers, then wake up.
4. Visualize the source where you are going to get the information; that is, imagine exactly how you will be told the numbers in your dream.
5. Think of a 'safe' place where you can travel in your dream to be made aware of the winning numbers.
6. Project some positive affirmations (e.g., love and well being to humanity) for good luck.

number came up. They were $100,000 richer.

"There must be a God because this is a miracle," the eldest son told reporters.

The Braggs put the money in the bank while they devised an investment strategy that would provide them with an income until Victor was ready to go back to work.

Talk about strange coincidences. Two women, both named Marie and living in Miami, chose the same set of lottery numbers in the same Kwik Stop convenience store on the same day in 1999. A few days later the women—who'd never met—shared a $15 million jackpot.

Luck was in the stars for Margaret Clemis of Burnaby, B.C.

In the spring of 1984, Margaret consulted a book of horoscopes to help her pick her Loto Canada ticket, and read that the best time for her to buy it would be between 4 and 6 p.m. on that Monday.

Margaret followed the instructions to the letter, and one week later collected a second prize check for $100,000. She'd never had much faith in astrology, she told the press. "But now, I believe."

Princess Caesar needed a little divine intervention. One frigid January day in 1997, she came home from work to find the door to her Brooklyn apartment padlocked. She and her 16-year-old daughter had been evicted. She managed to find a friend to take them in for the night. She prayed for a miracle and the next day it happened: Caesar won $4 million on the New York State lottery. She'd never have a problem paying her rent again.

If there's one thing that lottery winners have in common, it's that virtually all of them firmly believed that they would one day experience the luck of the draw. Irene Kangas is a case in point; she trusted her feelings, and ended up in our Lotto Hall O' Fame.

In the summer of 1991, this nurse from Sault St. Marie collected $13.9 million—the biggest single ticket win in Lotto 6/49 history.

"I feel very strongly that if you have a gut feeling then you should go with it," Irene said at her press conference. "I didn't feel that ticket specifically would win, but I've always felt when I bought tickets that whatever you give, you will eventually reap."

Irene and her husband Albert, a Bell Canada technician, had no plans on what to do with the money, although they hoped to take their children to Hawaii, just like they did in 1977, when they won a share of a $10,000 Wintario jackpot.

CHAPTER 11

WORK

If you want to get anywhere in this world, you have to work hard. Unless, of course, you're already rich. Or, you win the lottery.

Maria Grasso tried it the old-fashioned way. She'd worked hard all her life, struggling to raise her son and daughter. For a while, she had a job at a special school in Staten Island, New York, for children with cerebral palsy. Since 1996, she worked for millionaire venture capitalist Chris Gabrieli as a nanny for his four children. She lived a comfortable life, frequently sending any extra money she earned back home to her brothers and sister in Santiago, Chile. But on April 6, 1999, Grasso hit it big on the Big Game lottery, and when we say big we mean big. She was the single ticket-holder on a $197-million-dollar jackpot, a record unshared jackpot at that time, and still one of the biggest lottery pots ever. And one of Grasso's first thoughts, after the excitement of the lottery win had worn down? She was worried about her employer. She offered to work until he found a replacement, but Gabrieli just laughed. He urged her to take some time off to enjoy to her win and get used to having all that money.

And that's why most people buy tickets, isn't it? They dream of winning financial independence, and long for that moment when they can tell their boss to stick their job where the sun don't shine. And the beautiful thing about the lottery is that, sometimes, these dreams do come true, and often, even a modest jackpot is enough to make a hard-working person's life a little easier.

Of course, not everyone can win $197 million. But even those winners

LOTTERY GROUP AGREEMENT

When it come to lotteries, it only takes two to tangle. Take the story of two Des Moines, Iowa convenience store clerks. In February 1999, Timothy Schultz and co-worker Sarah Elder went halves on a Powerball ticket. Their numbers came up, but Schultz, who held the ticket, claimed the $28 million jackpot as his own. Elder sued. While the two were fighting it out in court, the Iowa lottery people asked the judge to declare the ticket sale illegal. The two parties quickly settled, agreeing to split the jackpot.

Fortunately, this sort of story is not that common. A lot of groups favor the subscription services offered in most states and provinces. With this service—which is available to individuals as well as groups—you prepay for up to one year of draws. For groups, it's a great way to play; you simple have to indicate on the form that you want a group subscription, and designate one person as group leader. The lottery people will automatically buy your group's tickets, check the numbers, and send you a check should you win.

Co-workers can avoid problems by filling out a group agreement. Most lottery corporations provide a form to groups who want a written record of their lottery pool. Here's a simple one that you can use with your group.

Please note, this is not a legal document, and we don't take any responsibility for problems that may arise should you score the jackpot. However, we'll gladly accept a portion of your winnings.

---

at the low end of the scale can find some peace of mind in their windfall. If anyone knows about hard work, it's Wilma Hugie and her husband Art. They've been farming just outside of Semans, 150 miles southeast of Saskatoon, Saskatchewan for over 35 years. They started off with a couple of quarters when they got married, and built their own two-room house. Within a few years, they had two sons and, bit by bit, added onto their home.

"After the boys grew up, they didn't really need me on the farm so much," Wilma says. "Then we had a crop failure and we needed the extra money, so I went and got me a job."

She found work at a nursing home in Strasburgh, 27 miles away. Every day for 14 years, she'd log over 50 miles on her commute. But even as the

GROUP LOTTERY FORM

We, the undersigned, have joined together in a group for the express purpose of purchasing lottery tickets. We agree to share any winnings equally, or as otherwise indicated on the "SHARE" section of this form.

NAME OF GROUP: (if applicable)

NAME(S) OF GROUP LEADER(S):
DATE:
PLAYER'S NAME:
GAME NAME:
DRAW DATE(S):
TICKET NUMBERS:
PLAYER'S NUMBERS:
PLAYER'S SHARE:
PLAYER'S SIGNATURE:

years passed, things did not get any easier for Wilma. The 1980s were hard on farmers everywhere, and over the last few years there was the added strain as her sons worked to take over the family farm. To help make ends meet, Wilma took another job working in a hospital laundry. It's been a long, often lonely haul for Wilma. Her one entertainment has been playing the lottery.

"I always get a few tickets," Hugie says. "My husband always used to ask me why I was spending my money on lottery tickets when I'd never win anything. But I'd say, it's the only thing I do other than work."

In August 1992, the Hugies took a Saturday off and drove into nearby Lumsden to see the rodeo. Wilma headed into town while her husband stayed to watch the races. She had a check she needed to cash, and besides, she always bought a lottery ticket on Saturday. The next day, she glanced at her ticket and noticed that she had one of the winning numbers; she figured she'd won ten dollars. Wilma dropped the ticket on an end table, and later stuck the ticket in her purse. She went to work on Monday morning as usual, and it wasn't until her afternoon break that she thought to look at her ticket again. That's when she realized she had two numbers, then three, then four, then five. . . . Wilma took her

SORRY, WRONG NUMBER

You've heard of employees who have to pay for their mistakes? Well, how about getting paid for them?

In the winter of 1988, Sue Zera hit the wrong number when she punched a ticket request into the computer. The customer refused to pay for the misnumbered tickets, and the Columbus, Illinois woman was forced to buy all 50 of them. Sue managed to sell 20 of the one-dollar tickets, but was stuck with a handful come draw day.

Guess what? One of the tickets turned out to be a $10 million winner. Now, that's the kind of mistake you can live with.

ticket to a drug store to get it verified.

"When they said that it was worth $97,400, I stood there like a frozen duck not knowing which way to turn. Then the girl came running over, saying that I didn't even seem excited. And I said, 'What's there to get excited about?' By that time, I was in shock. It seems like an impossible thing to have happen."

But reality hit her when she came back from Saskatoon a few days later with the check in her hand. "When I won, my husband and I weren't sure exactly what we were going to do. We weren't ready for retirement at the time, but we went on building a house. The lottery money didn't pay for it all, but it sure helped."

Along with the new home, Wilma was also able to set the farm's affairs straight. "We no longer need much more money, because everything will be paid. It's going to be tough for a little while, but the way were sitting right now, I've put a lot of money aside in RSPs, and I had gone with the matching pension from work. The way we're looking at it now, we should have a pretty good life going. The win came at a perfect time."

And as for work? Well, Wilma says that once she retires, she won't be doing anyone's laundry but her own. "It's time for a break, time to relax and enjoy what I've got left. Hopefully it's good health that both of us can enjoy."

While dreams of an early escape from work is one reason people play the lottery, it's also proved to be a way people who work together can play together. Office lottery pools are one of the most popular ways for people to take a chance on the luck of the draw. Take David Webb. He remembers the exact date: January 15, 1984. That's the day that he and three of his co-workers at the lab at the Halifax Infirmary Hospital

SILVER LININGS

Suzanne Kristie almost didn't buy that lottery ticket.

When she finally laid her money down for the July 11, 1990 draw, there were only minutes left before the computer system closed down.

Kristie, a single mother of two, had learned over the years to be very careful with her money. She'd struggled through years on welfare, eventually moving on to a series of low-paying jobs, until finally she was able to put herself through university. When she got her degree, she decided to try to help others; she worked as an outreach worker at the Boyle St. Co-op in Edmonton.

A few hours after she bought her ticket, Kristie's life took another turn for the better. In an instant, she found herself $10 million richer.

"In one fell swoop, as long as it took me to read those lottery numbers, all the doors I'd ever dreamed of flew wide open," Kristie told reporters at her press conference a few days later.

Kristie immediately quit her job, but didn't forget the hard times and struggles she'd faced. She pledged to contribute a portion of her winnings to worthy charities, including her old employer, the Boyle St. Co-op.

"I really believe that this money is a gift and that some of this money has to go back into the community."

joined forces in a Lotto 6/49 pool.

"We had these little sample cups that we numbered '1' to '49' and threw them in a paper bag, shook them up, and selected six sets of numbers. We stuck with them. We figured that you're going to increase your chances of losing if you switch your numbers each week."

Ten years later, they were still pooling their resources. Like a lot of people, they've found that when playing the lottery, the old adage "The more, the merrier" rings true. Audrey Skinner was one of David's poolmates. She thinks it was a great way to play.

"For one thing, it's cheaper. And you don't forget to get your tickets when you're in a pool—there's always somebody around to remind you. And it is more social than just playing by yourself."

David and Audrey were joined in their pool by co-workers Michael Graham and Clay Dymond. After picking their six sets of numbers, they continued to play them each, although they never developed an organized system for collecting money and buying tickets. As David explains,

WILL THE REAL LOTTERY WINNER PLEASE STAND UP?

 Add this to the lottery records held by groups: in March 1994, six employees of a Quebec grocery store shared a $19 million jackpot, the largest single ticket win in Canadian history. Each of the four men and two women collected $3.1 million.

However, their monumental win was overshadowed by a practical joke. Michel Beaulieu of Ste-Eustache, Quebec contacted the press to announce that he'd won the gigantic jackpot. As proof, he held up the winning ticket, with numbers clearly visible (although, he always seemed to have a finger covering the date).

But when he showed up at the Loto-Quebec office to collect, he revealed that it was all a hoax. He'd bought his ticket after the draw, using the winning numbers. It was all an April Fools' joke, he said, one that Michel hoped would snag him the $30,000 prize in a local radio station's crazy stunt contest.

How good was Michel's trick? Well, he had most of Quebec fooled, including Mario Sauve, one of the group who held the winning ticket. He'd already heard that someone had won the jackpot, and at first could not believe his own good fortune when he checked his ticket in the store's computer.

"I looked at the numbers," Mario told the press. "I told myself it can't be true. I checked again. Then I started to tremble."

they were all pretty casual about the whole thing.

"We just chipped in our share whenever it was due. I was the one who bought the tickets, for some reason, and I'm still doing it today with the same sets of numbers that we started out with."

Audrey points out that trust was central to their lottery group.

"I don't know what it would be like anywhere else. But we all worked together for twenty years, and we know one another really well. But if you don't know someone really well, maybe you should sign some forms ahead of time."

It sounds like a typical lottery group arrangement, just like the one you might belong to at your office or down at the bridge club. But it's not quite your average lottery pool. On January 15, 1989, exactly five years after she first agreed to play the lottery with her friends, Audrey got a phone call. It was David, who has a reputation as a bit of a kidder, to tell her that they'd won the lottery.

"I told him he was crazy and hung up the phone. And he called back and said, 'Would you just listen?'"

David recited the winning numbers—14, 21, 34, 40, 44, and 47—to Audrey.

"I still thought he was just kidding because anybody can tell you winning numbers and say he's got the ticket, but until you see it for yourself. . . ."

Then David called Mike, and Mike didn't believe him, either. But the next day at work, they got to see the ticket for themselves. They called the Atlantic Lottery Corporation hot line, and found out that they'd won a total of $1,241,144.80—good for more than $310,000 each. The following day, they flew to Moncton to collect their winnings. They kept the arrangement casual to the end, never actually formalizing their partnership.

"When we realized we won, we picked up some forms and brought them with us to the lottery office," Audrey says. "But, we worked together every day, so no one was going to try and skip off."

In fact, the thought of slipping out of town with the whole bundle did cross David's mind, but only for a second. "I could have had the whole shot. I had the ticket and realized that we had the winners. I had a decision to make: am I going to go to tell the rest of the guys about this, or am I going to cash it in and decide to live in Jamaica. . . ."

The final detail was to decide who would accept the winning check. It's standard practice that a jackpot check for a group win is made out to one specific person—otherwise, cashing it becomes a very complicated process. In this case, as Audrey explains, no one wanted the check.

"We knew at that time that anyone who had the check made out to them would be the one who got their name published in the papers and who got all the nuisance calls. Finally, Mike volunteered to do it."

Once they had the check in their hot little hands, David, Audrey, and company set off to the nearest bank, where they had the teller issue four separate certified checks. Then there was nothing left to do but fly back home to Halifax and spend the money. One of the first things they did was to put on a party for the rest of their hospital co-workers—all 120 of them. They rented a hall, and served free beer and pizza all night long. But all in all, they tried to keep level heads.

"Talk is cheap when the four of us are together," Audrey says. "But when it came down to reality, I think everybody just had to take a week and think, Well, I can't be crazy here. It took a while to sink in, and I don't think anybody did anything for a while."

David regarded his windfall with some caution.

"Sure, we won a little over a million, but we split that four ways. I try and put things in perspective here. When we won, I was trying to keep it on the quiet. You hear stories that people get hounded by insurance agents and salesmen—we weren't too bad off. It's just that people know that you've won, and it changes the way they look at you and talk to you. It changes your relationships."

How did they spend their cash? Well, David bought a new house and some furniture. But as Audrey says, the money doesn't last forever.

"Everybody thought it was a lot at the time, but it really wasn't. We all bought new cars, and I'm just buying a condo now. I didn't do anything special with mine: I gave away quite a bit, because I come from a big family. I had fun doing that."

They still play, following the same casual system they've always had. Along the way, they've won ten dollars here and there, which they always throw back in the kitty.

"And the rest of us still don't check numbers, we still depend on David. He's doing it all. As long as we have money in the pot he keeps buying tickets. When the money runs out, he asks for more."

It sounds like a great system. And, as long as no one catches David making plans for an extended holiday in Jamaica, one that should last them for years to come.

They called themselves Friends Forever, and the 17 co-workers at Kellogg Industries in Jackson, Michigan, were weeks away from being out of work together.

It was January 1997 and the workers had just heard that their plant was going to close its doors in the summer. Disheartened but not defeated, the co-workers formed the Friends Forever lottery club and pooled their resources. A few weeks later, the group hit it big, winning $45.6 million in the Big Game Lottery. The final tally: each member would receive $134,117.65 each year for the next 20 years. Talk about a golden handshake.

It seemed like a storybook tale.

In December 1981, an out-of-work Hamilton steelworker and father of three picked up the *Toronto Star* and checked the lottery numbers. At first, Brendan Foley couldn't believe his eyes. But there it was in black and white. His Provincial ticket had six of the seven numbers right, good for $50,000.

According to the *Montreal Gazette*, Foley believed he finally got the break he'd been looking for. He gave away his stereo and even his old Pinto, and made plans to move back to his native Newfoundland. To celebrate, he went to the race track and won $375 on a triactor. It was his lucky day indeed.

But that night when he got home, he was in for a shock. The paper had printed the wrong number.

"I felt sick," Foley told reporters, and who can blame him? There is a bright side, though; he did get rid of his Pinto.

In 1993, garbageman Albert Knight got his pick of the litter, bringing home a $5.9 million jackpot in the Maine lottery. Did he tell the boss to take his job and shove it? Nope. Knight, who appreciated the steady work after drifting from odd job to odd job for years, bought some new tires and a radio for the garbage truck, but stayed with his job.

"I promised myself I'd work for another two years," Knight told the press. "Besides, it keeps me out of mischief and from fighting with the old lady."

We all need co-workers like Jim Wingate. In 1995, Wingate, of Buffalo, New York, bought three tickets for himself and 83 lottery tickets for his work pool. The next day Wingate checked his tickets, but no luck. Then he checked the other tickets and realized that one of the pool tickets was worth $10 million. Thanks to Wingate's honesty, he and 16 co-workers will enjoy a $28,000 bonus each year for the next 20 years.

Claus Anthonisen didn't win the lottery: he *was* the lottery.

It was the summer of 1983, and the 19-year-old Winnipeg student had few job prospects. "He'd just finished his first year at McGill University," recalls his mother, Barbara. "He went down to the student employment office, and the kids were lined up around the block. The economy was pretty much a bust at the time, what with the recession and all."

Discouraged but not defeated, Claus came up with a novel solution: he decided to raffle himself off. What the heck; if governments could raise money through the lottery, why couldn't he?

So he had tickets printed, and sold them door-to-door for $5 each. Soon the local paper picked up the story, and gave Claus some much needed publicity. Within two weeks he reached his target: the money he collected was equal to what he would have earned working minimum wage for the summer.

At the last minute, it looked like Claus' enterprising plan would come crashing down when the lottery folks came calling, worried that his little scheme might be illegal.

"Claus said that he was selling tickets to raise money for educational purposes—he didn't say whose education."

The draw, held on June 1, was won by Elizabeth Jones of Winnipeg, a mother with two young children. She had lots of odd jobs for Claus: making a screen for her porch, painting the garage, putting up a fence, and helping to look after her two kids. But as Elizabeth confessed to a reporter at the time, watching Claus work so hard left her feeling a little uneasy.

"The poor kid was out in the back yard getting bitten by about eight million mosquitoes, and I'm in the house trying to read a book. So I just walked around the house feeling guilty."

All in all, Claus had a good summer, and proved that at least some of those lottery profits are put to good use.

Pierre-Thomas Girard of Montreal is one lottery winner who got to have his cake and eat it, too.

In January 1993, Pierre-Thomas was shopping on his day off when he picked up a Celebration ticket. It turned out to be a winner, and an unusual one at that.

"The Interprovincial Lottery Corporation was having a special promotion to celebrate their twentieth anniversary," Pierre-Thomas says. "I won a trip to Edmonton for the $1 million grand prize draw."

Pierre-Thomas got time off work and made the trip west, where he met up with 38 other finalists. He said that the televised draw was a nerve-wracking event.

"First, they drew ten balls to get ten finalists. My ball came up, and that got me $25,000. Then they drew six more balls, and my ball came out third again, and I picked up $50,000 more. They picked three balls; this time mine was first, and I won $100,000. That brought us to the final

THE OLD SOFT SELL

There's nothing like a little luck to change a man's heart. Arizona Judge David R. Cole, who was a vocal opponent to legalized gambling, denounced the state lottery when it started up in the 1980s. But in June 1996, Judge Cole was part of an office pool that won $12.5 million.

Five people in the office chipped in for the winning ticket, which caused the judge to promise to "re-evaluate" his opinion on lotteries.

draw, between me and two other players."

It seemed to take forever for the ball to roll out of the lottery draw machine, but exactly one minute and 56 seconds later, there it was: ball number 21, belonging to Pierre-Thomas.

All in all, Pierre-Thomas collected $1,175,000.

One of the first things he did after collecting his check was to check out of his job at H.B. Fuller, a glue company. It was a dream come true for Pierre-Thomas; now he had the time and resources to do whatever he wanted. But his life of leisure didn't last long. A few months after his win, he got a phone call.

"It was my old boss, asking me to come back to work. They couldn't find someone to replace me who could do the job as well as I had. It was a good feeling, and I did agree to go back, but this time, I was working on my terms."

Kenny Dukes is one lottery winner who'd like to quit his job. In 1995, Dukes won $31 million on the Georgia lottery. At the time, he was on parole from prison for a string of convictions that included breaking into his mother's trailer home and his father's truck. As a condition of his parole—which runs until 2002—Dukes must continue working.

"He's under the same conditions as any non-lottery winner on parole," his probation officer told the press.

Here's a tip: be careful when you accept a lottery ticket as a tip. As Tonda Dickerson found out, it can turn into a real pain in the butt. In 1999, Edward Seward Jr., a regular at the Grand Bay, Alabama, Waffle House where Dickerson worked, gave her a lottery ticket in lieu of a cash tip. Later that day, the numbers were drawn, and Dickerson found herself with a $10 million jackpot. But her co-workers called foul, and with Seward's support, took Dickerson to court, claiming that the ticket was meant to be split. The judge decided in their favor, and Dickerson saw her $10 million tip waste away to a paltry $2 million.

While work pools prove that there is strength in numbers, lottery clubs demonstrate the dangers of herd mentality (or, at the very least, that there is indeed a sucker born every minute). Rarely do you hear of any problems within pools, but as far as these so-called clubs go, problems seem to be the norm. What is a lottery club?

Basically, it's a mail-order outfit offering blocks of lottery tickets at highly inflated prices, anywhere from two to 20 times the ticket's face value. Most lottery clubs are based in Canada, but sell tickets in the U.S. and overseas—attracting customers with promises of huge lump-sum prizes, tax free (failing to mention that these are tax free in Canada only). Sometimes, the mail-order companies act as agents, purchasing specific lottery tickets for their foreign clients for a healthy fee.

In either case, you rarely end up with a ticket in your hand; the mail-order company hangs on to the tickets, and just sends you a confirmation of purchase. These mail order companies are legal in Canada, but not affiliated with any lottery corporation. However, it's actually illegal to send lottery tickets through the mail in the U.S.

For anyone foolhardy enough to try one of these lottery clubs, it might be a good idea to keep the story of Norman Gallagher in mind. Norman—"Chubby" to his friends—woke up on a Sunday in January, 1986, $10.2 million richer. His Lotto 6/49 ticket, with the numbers 12, 21, 24, 25, and 40, had been picked in the previous night's draw. Norman, who lived in Presque Isle, Maine, bought his winning ticket through Winshare, an Ontario-based company selling tickets on Canadian lotteries to Americans. A month earlier, he'd phoned in his order for several month's worth of draws. Although his order was three days past the normal deadline, the voice on the other end of the line assured him that there would be no problem. That took a load off his mind. He lived less than 15 miles from the Canadian border, but enjoyed the convenience of shopping for his lottery tickets by phone. He also didn't mind the extra expense; Norman paid two dollars U.S. for a ticket that normally sold for one dollar Canadian.

On Monday morning, Norman was in for the shock of his life. What could be bigger news than winning a fortune in the lottery? How about not winning a fortune in the lottery? As it turned out, Winshare did not process Norman's order. At first, they told him that the computer had rejected his credit card number, although later they told Norman's lawyer that the computer had malfunctioned.

"There's no way we could process his order," a spokesman for Winshare told the press. "It's a tough one. It's the one that got away."

Norman's story ends here, but it's not the last word on Winshare. Two days later, papers around the country were reporting that a certain Esther Budharam had won over 80 lottery prizes over the previous five years, for a total of almost a quarter of a million dollars. Coincidentally, Esther was married to Ernest Priess, sole director of the Winshare Club of Canada. Other Winshare employees had collected prizes up to $15,000.

Ernest Priess dismissed the wins as sheer luck.

"Anybody can win lots of money depending on two things—their luck and how much they spend," Priess told the *Globe & Mail*. He added that any hint of wrongdoing was the result of an ongoing feud he was having with lottery officials.

"This is an absolutely zero issue. The Ontario Lottery Corp. will intentionally slant things and try and make me and my wife look bad. . . . I showed them conclusively there is no way Mr. Gallagher's ticket was ordered by us, or that any money changed hands or that it could have been processed on time."

In the long run, nothing changed through this battle of words; Norman Gallagher remained—like most of us—someone who woke up from a wonderful dream, only to find that he'd come up short in the luck of the draw.

The story of Blair Down proves that Gallagher's bad luck was no fluke. Until February 1999, this Vancouver-based realtor and his company Crystal Communications were pulling off the lotto scam of a century. Preying on elderly Americans, Down's company would sell "shares" in his ticket club; winnings would be reinvested and the money would accumulate over time. It sure did; by the time police caught up with Down, he'd sweet-talked seniors out of $210 million. Fortunately, Down went down, but lottery scams continue to this day. You can bet your last dollar on that.

CHAPTER 12

SPORTS

Sports and lotteries. They go together like chickens and suspenders. It seems that when government-sponsored lotteries try to get into the sports betting game, things often go amiss.

There have been sports stars who have been on the winning end of lotteries themselves. Maybe the most famous one ever to win big on the lottery—the biggest celebrity of any kind—was Hollywood Henderson. Thomas Hollywood Henderson always did things in a big way. When he was a star linebacker with the Dallas Cowboys and Houston Oilers back in the 1970s, he loved the limelight. And even when he crashed, he did it in a big way. In 1979, the Cowboys cut Henderson because of his crack-cocaine addiction. Four years later, Henderson wound up in prison after police found him smoking crack with two teenage girls. He'd threatened the girls with a gun, the police said, and sexually assaulted one of them. He did just over two years in jail, and came out a changed man.

Flash forward to the year 2000. Henderson was still living in Austin, Texas, where he'd spent most of his life. He'd given up drugs, and spent much of his time giving motivational speeches and doing community work. Despite his addiction, Henderson hadn't squandered all his earnings. On May 24, 2000, Henderson went to Nau's Drugs, a local pharmacy, and lay down $100 for tickets on the state lottery. He wasn't a regular player, but liked to try his luck whenever the jackpot went over $20 million. The next day he checked his numbers against the draw: 5, 8, 17, 35, 38, and 41. He had them all, along with a $28 million jackpot. His life had

THAT'S THE WAY THE BALL BOUNCES

The biggest lottery story of 1994 had nothing to do with multi-million dollar jackpots—an indication of how much the lottery in Canada was changing. The issue was before the courts; the basketball courts, that is. The story centered around the U.S.-based National Basketball Association and its announced plan to create franchises in Vancouver and Toronto. It was a done deal, according to the NBA. All that was needed was an agreement from the British Columbia and Ontario governments to remove NBA games from their sports betting pools. . . .

At first, the provinces cried foul. No hot-shot American sports league was going to dribble onto our home court and tell us how to run our business, they said. The NBA's position—shared by other leagues who find their games fodder for provincial betting pools—is that the association with gambling taints their sport. More to the point, the NBA maintained that it held the copyright over any and all things to do with their league, including schedules and game scores.

It was a tense shootout that threatened to go into overtime. But at the last minute, after the story had been milked for every drop of publicity, the two sides came to terms. The provinces promised to drop the NBA from its sports pool, in return for a little cash: Ontario would get $12 million, B.C., $2.5 million.

come full circle: Hollywood Henderson was on top again.

"I'm just going to continue to do the charities I do, take care of my children, and buy my momma a Town Car," Henderson told the press after a celebration breakfast of powdered doughnuts and milk. "Today I know how to handle success, and that's important."

So much for sports winners. When it comes to losers—well, that seems to be lottery players in general whenever governments decide to dip their feet into the sports betting pool. Canadian lotteries have a particularly bad track record when it comes to sports betting. The very first legal lotteries in Canada were aimed at reducing the debts incurred by the 1976 Summer Olympics in Montreal.

These early attempts at sports-based lotteries were disastrous. Some of them even tried to incorporate a sports theme into the mix. In 1981, Lotto-Quebec initiated Loto-Hockey, perhaps one of the most stupid lotto games ever. To win, all players had to do was predict the exact moment, in minutes and seconds, of hockey goals and penalties. Simple,

PARLEZ-VOUS SPORTS BETTING?

So your menu has a low line? Sounds all Greek to you? In fact, the language of sports lotteries is quite simple, once you get the hang of it. There are basically two types of bets allowed: "parimutuel," also called "oddset," and "over/under." In the first, players have to predict the outcome—selecting the winning team or a tie—in at least three specific games. There are pre-set odds which determine how much a player will win if correct.

In "over/under," players bet against the predicted total points in a single game. For example, if Sports Action predicts that Toronto and Montreal will score a total of 11 goals in a specific hockey game, you bet either "over" (if you think they'll score more than 11 goals) or "under" (if you think they'll score less).

The "line" is a gambler's term which refers to the odds or the total point score offered by the lottery corporation. The "menu" is a weekly listing of upcoming games and lines, put out by the lottery corporation. A "low" or "soft" line means that on a given game, either the odds are unusually high or the point total is unusually low—which is good news for the bettor.

right? Not surprisingly, the game lasted less than a year. The following season, Quebec tried Hockey-Select, a simpler game, but still one that required players to predict the outcome of 13 games. Hockey-Select lasted one year, with total sales of less than $1.6 million. The problem with these games is that they were either too confusing to play, or seemed too difficult to win. There was also a legal issue. Lotteries were, by definition, games of chance, while sports bets required a degree of skill; since they were not games of chance, they were technically illegal.

Lottery corporations avoided sports betting altogether until 1988 when British Columbia, encouraged by some successful sports lotteries in the U.S., launched a Canadian Football League pool. The next year, B.C. found even greater success with a Super Bowl lottery, and by the 1990s, sports lotteries were an established niche game. They appealed to a very specific audience: men, usually young, who already enjoyed betting the odd dollar on a Saturday night's game.

Take Lui Jurinak, for example. He knows a good thing when he sees it. That's why he got excited when he picked up the B.C. Lottery Sports Action "menu" late in October 1994.

A Hockey Team by Any Other Name . . .

 Ever notice how most sports lotteries never list a team's full name, or the name of the actual sports league? For example, a game between the Toronto Maple Leafs at home against the Dallas Stars would be classified on the menu only as a hockey game played between Toronto and Dallas.

This is how the folks at your local lottery corporation get around the issue of copyright infringement. In fact, they could be talking about any game between any Toronto and Dallas teams.

"The B.C. Lottery was offering ridiculously low lines. The games were all NBA pre-season, which are notoriously high scoring anyway. And that year they had got new rules in the NBA, designed to make the game even more offence-oriented."

Lui was so excited that he convinced five friends to join him in the hunt for the Big Score. "We all chipped in $5,000 each, and keyed our money on certain games. We had a system designed to get us our maximum pay-out, which means we weren't just playing the safest games."

Since $100 is the highest bet Sports Action would accept, Lui and his friends bought hundreds of tickets, of various game combinations, but always betting higher scores than Sports Action's. "Since the total points in each game offered by the lottery company were so low, we bet 'over' in every game, meaning we thought the teams would score more points than the lottery corporation predicted."

Although Lui describes himself as a sports fan who's good with numbers and knowledgeable about sports betting, he says he rarely plays the lottery sports pools.

"It's not a good bet. You're better off going down to Las Vegas and putting money on a single football game, than betting in this type of situation where you have to get at least three game scores right. It's hard enough to get one game score; the more games, it just becomes harder and harder."

While he says that no intelligent gambler would normally lay down money on a lottery pool, occasionally opportunity comes knocking. And on this particular day, opportunity seemed to be using both fists on the door. One of the people Lui Jurinak talked into taking a chance on Sports

HELPING THE NEEDY

The province of Manitoba came up with a sporting way to spend some of its video lottery terminal earnings in 1994. The government awarded a meager $5.2 million to the needy players and club directors of the Winnipeg Jets hockey team—barely enough money to cover Teemu Selanne's contract. The idea was to try to keep pro hockey in Winnipeg, but it didn't work. The owners turned around and sold the team a few seasons later to new owners who moved it to Phoenix, but kept their lottery windfall.

In the same breath, the Manitoba government admitted that it had earmarked almost $1 million in lottery revenues to a program designed to maintain the opulent lifestyle of 350 unemployed students.

"Lottery revenues must be used to the best possible benefit for all Manitobans," Finance Minister Eric Stefanson proudly declared at the time. Undoubtedly, overworked and underpaid professional hockey players throughout the province breathed a huge sigh of relief. It's just another example of your voluntary tax dollar at work.

Action was his buddy, Sal Guzzo. Unlike Lui, Sal was just a casual sports fan. He played Sports Action every once in a while, never betting more than $100. But when he saw the odds for the NBA pre-season games, it was an opportunity he couldn't pass up.

"The lottery corporation just threw these games out because they had nothing else out to bet on. There was no hockey, there was really nothing; so they thought, 'Let's see if we can get some action.' But the games they chose were so unpredictable, not even Las Vegas was offering odds on them."

Like a hot stock market tip, word of Sports Action's mistake spread like wildfire through Vancouver, and by that Tuesday, ticket sales had increased 600 percent.

At noon on Tuesday, the B.C. Lottery Corporation suspended play on the NBA "over/under" game. Mobsters, they feared, were laundering money through it. "Sales have been unusually high and it's difficult to think that it was just disposable income," a BCLC spokeswoman told the *Vancouver Sun* at the time.

GAME OVER

 Christmas came a little late for soccer fans at Feathers, a British-style pub in Toronto, and the Ontario Lottery Corporation played the part of jolly old St. Nick.

The fans won more than $800,000 by betting on the outcome of English First Division soccer matches in Ontario's Pro-Line sports lottery early in January 1995. The bets were a "sure thing," not because the teams were grossly mismatched, but because the OLC accepted wagers for an hour and a half after the last game ended.

"It was our mistake," a spokesman for the lottery corporation told the press. "We should have closed off games at 10 a.m. rather than 2 p.m."

Talk about your Christmas turkey. . . .

Lui and his friends were outraged. "Their story about mobsters is just a crock," Lui says. "They knew they made a mistake, and they just didn't want to have to pay out. It was just a move to save their asses."

Sal agrees. "The lottery was just looking for some action. They got it big then they said, 'Forget it, we don't want it any more.' Then they didn't even have the guts to say that they made a mistake. I mean, if you were a mobster, would you bet your money on a game?"

Sal and Lui are right. The BCLC's money-laundering story does sound a little fishy. While there have been some problems with drug dealers and other unsavory characters laundering money through lotteries, they usually do so by buying winning tickets at above the prize value—and this practice usually takes place outside of Canada. In fact, a few months before the basketball foul-up, a BCLC spokesperson scoffed at stories of people laundering money through a lottery.

"Logistically, I can't imagine it," the spokesperson told a *Vancouver Sun* reporter. "We don't even know who has a winning ticket until a winner comes forward."

Disillusioned with the BCLC, and upset with the implication that they might be mobsters, Sal and Lui took their story to CKVU, a local television station.

"They came to our place so we could show them that we're not mob-

MOB RULES POOLS

You think it's tough to win a hockey pool these days? Try playing them thirty years ago.

According to a 1961 *New York Times* report, Canadian sports pools were a big, bad business. The mobsters who ran the illegal racket racked up sales of 1 million tickets a week in Montreal alone, raking in $25 million each year from pollsters across the country.

A one-dollar ticket earned you a chance at a $400 payday; all you had to do was guess the exact time of the final goal of the game. While the hockey pool provided a healthy source of income to the criminals who organized it, the lottery proved unhealthy for anyone foolish enough to cross them. In the first three months of the year, police found four bullet-ridden bodies, victims of the gangland politics of Canada's first sports lottery.

sters," Sal says. "To show them that we're just local players who had a break, a Christmas present—that's what we called it. And the lottery corporation took that dream away from us."

Despite BCLC's move, which prevented any more ticket sales, Lui, Sal, and the boys still had $30,000 riding on those NBA pre-season games. If everything went their way, they stood to win more than $2 million. As luck would have it, everything came down to the final game. Portland was playing Golden State in a game that, Sal believes, should have been a high-scoring affair.

"We watched the game together. One of my friends has a big satellite. We even phoned down to Portland at half time to ask them, 'Please, can you get your players to play the game. We've got too much money riding here.' We called the announcer. He said it was the worst game he had ever seen when it came to baskets."

The final score was under the BCLC predicted line; it was the only game that didn't go over. "We should have been smarter. Once they make a mistake like that, you can't leave everything to the final game. I think there was greed on our part, too. We saw that money. We saw the mistake, we wanted the money; but they made a big mistake and should have paid for it."

Sal Guzzo and friends were not the first to complain about B.C.'s Sports Action lottery.

In September 1991, Victoria, B.C.'s Terry Volb found that there were limits as to how far the sports pool would let players go. Terry discovered that bets with odds of 5,000 to one or better are automatically rejected by the game computer. The odds were set by the B.C. Lottery Corporation. According to a story in Victoria's *Times-Colonist*, Terry then phoned the BCLC to find out what was going on.

"They said if I wanted to make a lot of money I should play the 6/49," Terry told the paper. "I'm thinking of getting hold of hockey analyst Don Cherry and telling him what sort of game he's being spokesman for."

Apparently, Sports Action was not in the business of making players rich, as a spokesman for the lottery corporation made clear at the time. "With a little skill and a little risk you can make a reasonable win, but as far as creating a long shot, there's the 6/49."

And just to prove that some things never change, the Ontario Lottery Corporation has kept the tradition of big time sports bet welching alive. In one classic case, the lottery company closed bets on its popular Pro-Line sports lottery at the eleventh hour. The game requires players to predict the winners of hockey, football, and baseball games. Officials got a little nervous when they actually calculated their net loss if three big NHL underdogs—Anaheim, Tampa, and Nashville—pulled off upsets. Not wanting to risk going into the red, officials simply stopped taking bets. But that was par for the course for a corporation that had already deemed overtime wins in hockey to be ties—which carry a much lower pay-out. Not bad for a company that regularly nets about $200 million a year on sports lotteries, paying out only about $115 million in prizes.

It was supposed to be Ottawa's Golden Goose, the game that would lead the federal government back into the lottery gravy; instead, it turned into the Golden Turkey. From May to September of 1984, the federal Canadian Sports Pool Corporation, SportsSelect's overseer, managed to run up $46 million in losses—earning the distinction of being the biggest flop in Canada's lottery history.

Originally, Ottawa hoped SportsSelect would raise $400 million for the 1988 Winter Olympics in Calgary. But when Canada's Liberal government announced the lottery early in 1984, the provinces were outraged. The feds had signed an agreement in 1979 promising to keep their big snout out of the lottery trough. In return, the provinces paid the feds $24 million a year. Ottawa countered by saying that SportsSelect involved some skill—a debatable point at best—and was therefore not a lottery. In

March, in a last-ditch effort to stop the sports pool, the provinces took Ottawa to court.

Meanwhile, the American government was leaning on Canada to stop the SportsSelect pool. Washington launched an official complaint with the Canadian ambassador to the U.S. over the use of baseball scores in the betting pool. Even Bowie Kuhn, baseball's colorful commissioner, got into the act, threatening that the sports pool would kill Vancouver's bid to get a professional baseball team. Despite the adversity, the Canadian government gamely persevered and in May held their first SportsSelect draw.

Four months later, the lottery was losing a million dollars a week, and had yet to award a jackpot prize. In a federal election held on September 4, the Liberals suffered a resounding defeat at the hands of Brian Mulroney's Conservatives. When the Tories assumed power ten days later, their first piece of business was to axe the SportsSelect Baseball Pool. Why did the sports pool fail so wonderfully? Ken Kalino has a theory.

"It was stupid," says the 44-year-old Montrealer. "The game itself was pretty complicated, and the odds were something like 89 million to one. No wonder nobody played it."

This isn't a case of sour grapes. Kalino shared, with a dozen co-workers, the $4.8 million jackpot in the final SportsSelect draw on September 30, 1984. Unlike pool games today, which allow players a lot of freedom to pick teams and scores, SportsSelect was very rigid. Players paid two dollars for a ticket bearing 13 pre-printed baseball game outcomes. The first four game results were visible; the other nine were hidden, and players had to scratch to find out what they were. To win the jackpot, the outcome of 13 real-life baseball games had to match a player's ticket.

To make things even more difficult, there were only three possible outcomes for every game: home team wins by one run; home team loses by one run; home team wins by more than one run. In other words, if any team in the pool of 13 games lost at home by more than one run, a player had no chance to win the jackpot. No wonder SportsSelect became known as the game nobody could win.

"We only played it that one time," Ken Kalino says. "We heard that it was the last draw, and that if no one won the jackpot they were going to give the money to the next highest winners, so we figured what the hell. . . ."

Kalino and his co-workers at Mint Master, a Montreal precious metal trading company, bought a series of 170 tickets and waited to see what would happen. Meanwhile, the organizers of SportsSelect kept bungling right down to the wire. Days before the deadline, the lottery corporation took out ads in major newspapers enticing people to buy tickets, even though by that time 95 percent of retailers had sold all their tickets. And speaking of retailers, those corner store and kiosk owners who'd decided to sell sports pool tickets found themselves high and dry in the end. . . .

The final baseball games in the pool were played on a Sunday. The following day, Kalino went in to work early to check their tickets. He didn't even have money enough that morning to pay for his parking. "I told the guy I'd see him at the end of the day."

Kalino and co-worker Michelle Laflamme start to scratch and check for winning tickets. They'd already gone through nearly 50 of them when he came across one ticket with four correct scores showing.

"I scratched and saw that we had the right score for the first hidden number. Then I scratched again and soon we were up to eight right scores. I said, 'Hey, we've won a hundred bucks.' I kept scratching, past nine, then ten. That's when it started to get a bit dicey. We started scratching slower. Then we got to twelve; there was one left, and we still had it. I wanted to wait for the rest of the people to show up, but Michelle said no."

Carefully, Kalino scraped off the latex to reveal the last remaining score. It matched.

"Michelle actually passed out and fell off her chair. I helped her up and said, 'Let's open the petty cash.' By that time it was nine-thirty, so I went over to the liquor commission and bought four bottles of champagne. We partied all that day; I don't even think we opened the doors."

Not everybody at Mint Master was overjoyed. One unlucky employee had passed on his opportunity to buy into the ticket pool.

"He said he'd rather buy a case of beer; that was his quote. You should have seen his face when I told him we'd won; I felt so sorry for him. They came around afterwards to ask everyone to make a donation, to give him money. I didn't give him a cent. This guy had a chance to go in, and he didn't want to go in. I even told him that I didn't give him any. He still got $40,000, believe it or not, from the other people."

Kalino's cut of the SportsSelect win was a cool $285,500. He told reporters that he had no plan to quit his job, and when asked what he planned to do with his winnings he said he'd probably blow $30,000 and invest the rest. But, as Kalino told me in a recent interview, things turned out rather different than planned.

"Some people win the lottery and don't even go to McDonald's, but that's not the way I live. I mean, if you win the lottery, why just put it all away in the bank? If you won a car in a lottery, would you just park it in a garage all the time?"

The first thing he did was to take ten friends on a trip to Barbados. He also restored his 1972 Triumph TR6, gave money to his sisters and brothers, and sent his mom on a trip . . . up the Amazon River.

"She was sixty then. She'd never been outside North America. And when I asked her where she wanted to go on vacation she said some place like Atlantic City or Miami. And I said, 'Come on! You can go anywhere.' So she told me to pick a place for her. I went to a travel agent, who showed me a brochure for this Amazon cruise, and I knew that would be perfect for my mom. She had the time of her life."

Kalino stayed with Mint Master for a while, then took a couple years off before starting an import/export business with a friend. "We did okay. We broke even, and the only reason was because we had the money to put up front. But we broke even in the end."

Almost a year after the final SportsSelect draw, Ottawa and the provinces reached an agreement. The federal government promised to stay out of the lottery business forever. In return, the provinces would cough up $100 million over the next three years. In other words, the five provincial lottery corporations paid the federal government millions and millions of dollars to stop running a money-losing lottery. This was in addition to the fact that the provinces were already shelling out $36 million every year under the terms of the 1979 agreement.

Meanwhile, Kalino now owns a courier business. He doesn't have a lot left to show for his lottery win, but figures he had a pretty good run. "I could have bought a couple of houses, or other investments. But that's not what I wanted to do. I bought some land. I spent most of it, and I had a good time. It was the greatest thing that ever happened to me—I was given $200,000 for nothing. It enabled me to do things I would have never been able to do."

Of course, he still plays the lotteries, buying a couple of 6/49 tickets each week. And he has no delusions about what he'll do if he ever wins the Big One.

"I don't believe it when people say that winning a million dollars wouldn't change their life. That's b.s. It has to change you. I tell you what I really don't understand—people who win a million dollars then say I'm going to work Monday! I win a million dollars, I'm gone; you won't see me again."

CHAPTER 13

SCRATCH AND LOSE

Got the lottery itch? Try scratching.

What started off as a bonus premium on draw-style lottery games has evolved into one of the most popular forms of lottery today.

What's the attraction? First of all, they offer instant gratification, or instant disappointment; you don't have to wait, heaven forbid, one or two days to find out if you've won. They also generally offer a much better chance than any other kind of lottery for players to win something; although the jackpots are limited, usually in the $10,000 to $50,000 range, you often have a better than 50 percent chance of getting your money back or, at least, a free ticket.

To sweeten the deal, some provinces are now offering $1 million instant win tickets, with odds on winning the jackpot that are much more attractive than the 14-million-to-one shot players take on Lotto 6/49. A recent Ontario Instant Millions, for example, offered five $1 million top prizes. The Ontario Lottery Corporation calculated the chances of coming away a big winner one in 1.6 million.

Steve Culp of Drayton, a town 25 minutes east of Kitchener, Ontario, is one man who tried his luck on an instant win ticket. Back in the winter of 1996, when he was 24, Steve bought a five-dollar Ontario Instant Millions ticket at a local variety store. He usually buys some kind of ticket every day. Steve took the ticket to the local arena where he's a maintenance worker. He liked to savor his instant win tickets, so he didn't look at it until after lunch, taking care to scratch one number at a time.

"To win the jackpot on this ticket, you have to match three of the 'one

---

I'VE WON! NOW WHAT?

Steve Culp wasn't sure what to do after his million dollar scratch. Would you know what to do if you won? The first thing is to sign the back of your lottery ticket, and fill in your name, address, and phone number. It's also a good idea to make a photocopy of both sides of your ticket, and put it away in a safe place. Then if you lose your ticket, or if someone steals it, you should still be able to collect.

Your next step is to get your money. Contact your state or provincial lottery company to find out the best way to collect in your area.

---

million dollar' signs. I scratched two 'million dollar' signs off right away."

But he didn't get too excited, since other times he'd played he'd often scratched two 'million dollar' signs. "I left one row to the last, but I accidentally scratched part of that row too, and noticed part of a letter instead of a number sign. I started to shake and shiver, and then I scratched the rest of it, and there it was."

Steve ran out to the ice rink, where his brother was playing hockey. "He couldn't believe it. So I went there, and my father happened to be home, so I showed him and he got excited. I didn't know what to do right away, so we found out how late the lottery office in Toronto would be open, and then my cousin drove me down in my truck."

They got to the lottery office 15 minutes before closing time. By five o'clock, Steve was back on the road, a $1 million check in his pocket.

"They said it normally takes forty-five minutes to get the check through and authorized, but it didn't even take fifteen minutes for me. I've got a little tip for people: if anyone wins, they should go down to collect shortly before five."

Steve booked off work for a couple of days to get his affairs in order. He talked to a lawyer, and sought the advice of a financial planner. A few days later, he was back at work.

"Everybody says, what are you still doing working? But, I just couldn't leave right away. There's only three of us working in the arena over the winter—it was still in the winter time when I won—so I just couldn't go and leave two of them stranded there. Besides, if I quit, I'd sit around and do nothing. I love hockey, so being in the arena is ideal for me. I can watch people play, I can go up and play myself whenever I want."

Steve has promised to stay at least one more year on the job. After that, who knows? "I've always liked go-carting, so I may look into starting

DON'T TAKE ANY WOODEN TICKETS

Most lottery corporations leave instant win tickets in circulation even after all the prizes are won, so theoretically the scratch ticket you buy has absolutely no chance of winning. It's a good idea to check the lottery office to see if there are still prizes left—particularly major prizes—before you buy any tickets on a scratch-and-win game that has been out for a while. Also, don't buy seasonal tickets after the season has clearly past. In other words, if you picked up a Halloween-themed scratch-and-win ticket just in time for Mother's Day, you're probably out of luck.

a go-cart track. Or a driving range. . . ."

But just because Steve is keeping his job doesn't mean he hasn't enjoyed his win. The first thing he did was to go out and buy himself a couple nice 'toys': an 18 1/2 foot fishing boat, and a Chevy 4x4 truck. He gave his old truck, purchased two years earlier, to his brother, and bought a loaded van for his parents. Did he have to buy a round of beer for his friends as well?

"Actually, no. Most of my friends that I went to school with don't live around here now. There's my brother's buddies; I hang around with them a bit. They tease me once in while about the win. I say, oh well, If you scratch, you might win, too."

Like most winners, Steve kept playing after he scratched his jackpot. At first, he says, he hardly bought any tickets at all. But now, he's back to his old routine of buying a ticket a day.

"I actually enjoy playing as much as I enjoy winning. I love scratching. I take my time. I scratch one box. I may scratch the top line off first, then the bottom line, the last line. It's just something I enjoy."

Under the 'I'—instant win!

Bingo games are one of the most popular types of instant win tickets. Every province has at least one scratch-and-win variation on this classic church hall game.

Just like in real bingo, players try to complete rows on their "bingo card." Each ticket has at least one of these "cards" printed on it. (Many tickets carry more than one card.) Players scratch the "caller's card" to determine what numbers to mark on their "players card."

It's easier than it sounds. Two years ago, Doris Glushyks, a waitress from Melford, Saskatchewan, bought a scratch bingo ticket. She's the type of player who buys tickets once in a while, whenever the mood strikes her. Doris picked up her ticket on the way home from a 12-hour shift at the Hi-Lo Motel. She came in the door, turned on the TV, and put her feet up. Then she started to scratch her ticket.

"At first, I thought I'd won $1,000. Then I double-checked and realized I'd won $10,000! I couldn't talk. It just kind of stunned me, and because I live alone, I had nobody to scream at. I kept thinking, What if I'm not seeing right?"

Doris phoned her daughter in nearby Kenora.

"She asked me what was wrong, and I told her that I thought I'd just won a lot of money. She was more excited than me."

The $10,000 windfall came in pretty handy for Doris. She paid off some bills, got a badly-needed paint job for the car, gave some to her kids, then took a trip to visit her daughter in North Carolina—and still managed to squirrel away some cash.

The news of the win spread like wildfire through the small town of Melford, and within hours it seemed like everyone had heard the news. Most people were happy for her, but she did get some negative comments. One person, who didn't identify himself, called her and asked how the "rich bitch" was doing. There was even a little incident on her next trip to the store to buy lottery tickets.

"I was in line for a ticket, when a man behind me piped up, 'Don't be so greedy, you've already had your win.' When I heard that I stepped back and said, 'You go ahead first, I'll let you get the lucky one.'"

Despite a couple of bad experiences, Doris is still happy about her bingo win. In fact, it started a little trend. One week after calling "Bingo," she picked up $1,000 on Lotto 6/49.

"They say that good luck comes in threes. When I won $10,000 on the Bingo, not even a week later I played the 6/49 and I got the last five on the extra, and I won $1,000. I'm still waiting for my third big win."

It's funny how things work out.

When Chris phoned Margaret Currie of Sydney, Nova Scotia, for example, he expected to talk to the woman who'd been the first $1 million dollar winner of the Atlantic Lottery Corporation's Provincial/Super Lotto draw. Instead, he got a different Margaret Currie, who had also won a big lottery prize. It was back in 1987, and Margaret was down to her last two dollars.

"My sister was running a restaurant at that time, BJ's Diner, and as I was leaving, I just said to her, 'Give me two of those Tic Tac Toe tickets.'"

SNEAK PREVIEWS

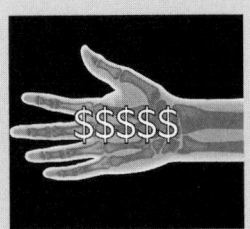

Ever wished you had x-ray vision? That way, you could go into your local variety store, glance at a row of instant win tickets, and spot the million dollar winner. Actually, you don't need superhuman powers; a 100-watt light bulb just might do the trick. At least, that's what Bill Chowen of London, Ontario discovered. Back in July 1984, Chowen noticed that his Wintario ticket was unusually thin. On a whim, he held it up to a high-powered light bulb and, low and behold, he could make out the words beneath the scratch-out portion of the ticket.

In that particular ticket series, the words "Good Luck!" were printed on the bonus scratch section, and players could earn five free tickets to go along with the regular draw. Thanks to Chowen's sharp eyes, and his quick call to the OLC, lottery officials responded to the see-through scratches before they had a major problem on their hands. But this incident is small potatoes compared to the Great Provincial Peek-a-boo Ticket Scandal in the winter of 1987.

Again, the tool of choice was a high intensity lamp, and the object of interest was a special series of the Provincial, which came packaged with a bonus ticket, worth up to $5,000, in a sealed pouch. Some enterprising folk discovered that when these flimsy pouches were held up to the light, they could read the bonus ticket.

But here's the twist. Some of these curious people worked for Lotto Quebec. They spent hours checking tickets before they were even put into distribution, and were able to set aside $30,000 worth of tickets for themselves—just in time for Christmas. In January of the following year, ten people were arrested, including two Lotto-Quebec employees, after police heard that one of the employees had been bragging about the scam. Sales of Provincial tickets were also halted—although lottery officials promised to honor any winning tickets already purchased.

So go ahead, give this simple ticket test a try. All you need is a willing merchant, a high-powered light, and a very long extension cord.

DON'T SCRATCH THAT ITCH

Oscar Wilde once said that he could resist anything but temptation, and the same sentiments apply to a least one young scratch-and-win player.

In the summer of 1988, Debbie (not her real name) showed up for her overnight shift at the Mac's Milk convenience store in Cornwall, Ontario. Everything was going fine, until she decided to try her hand on a couple of instant win tickets. She didn't win a thing, then realized that she also didn't have any money to pay for her scratch attack. In desperation, she scratched ticket after ticket, looking for that elusive big win.

A few hours and 127 tickets later, Debbie gave up, and dumped the losing tickets into the dumpster, where her boss discovered them the next morning. Debbie got a suspended sentence and six months probation, proving once again that crime, just like lotteries, doesn't always pay.

Tic Tac Toe is one of the most popular kind of instant win tickets, and almost all of Canada's provincial lottery corporations offer a variation on this simple game: scratch your ticket to see if you have a row of Xs or Os, and if you do, scratch another box to see how much you've won.

Margaret scratched her first ticket.

"Ma, you just won $10,000," her oldest son, who was watching, said.

Doris thought he was kidding. "Go away, Freddy, you're crazy."

"Ma, put your glasses on, you just won $10,000."

Margaret put her glasses on, and found that she had indeed won ten grand.

"I couldn't believe it. I handed the ticket to my husband, and before I knew it the ticket went all around the restaurant. Somebody asked me where my ticket was; I had no idea. . . ."

Back then, Atlantic lottery winners had to travel to Moncton, New Brunswick to collect their prizes. For Margaret and her husband Basil, that meant a ten-hour drive, but it was a trip they were happy to make.

"I wish I had been the $1 million winner. That would have been nice. But I was very satisfied with my $10,000, believe me. It was like a million to me at the time; it paid off my house and paid off a lot of other little piddly things."

And as it turned out, the win proved to be very timely for Margaret.

"I always said that God gave me that money because two years later my husband was diagnosed with cancer." Basil died in 1989.

Today, Margaret still likes the lotto. She plays Lotto 6/49 on a regular basis, but her favorite remains the instant games. "I play all the time. I never go past a booth unless I buy one or two tickets. I like the scratch ones the most because I don't like waiting to see if I won. And, I'm still hoping for the big one."

Here's another hot lotto tip: try moving to Curno, a small town in northern Italy. In 1996, the national lottery corporation accidentally printed too many winning tickets on its *Sette e Vinci*—"Seven and Win"— scratch card; and by mistake, the cards were actually shipped to retailers. It seems most of the winning cards made their way to Curno and other small towns in the province of Bergamo. In the span of a few weeks, townspeople won more than $3.2 million.

In November 1999, the *New York Daily News* discovered that the lottery business isn't as easy as it looks. In an effort to raise its circulation, the newspaper ran a scratch-and-win-style contest. But it mistakenly printed the wrong winning numbers, causing thousands of readers to believe they'd won cash prizes up to $100,000. To make amends, the paper ran a separate sweepstakes just for readers who'd been misled by the original game.

CHAPTER 14

CASINO ROYAL

Friday of every month, Anthony gets off work a little early, jumps in his car, and starts the two-and-a-half hour trek from Toronto to the Windsor Casino, just across the river from Detroit. Windsor is Canada's gambling capital. In fact, for a while in the mid-1990s, it was America's gambling capital, too, as long line-ups of American tourists stretched around the block to take a chance on the only legal gambling facilities within driving distance.

"It's my little getaway; it's how I keep myself sane," Anthony says. "I set a strict budget and I stick to it. I stay Friday night until Sunday morning, and I allow myself $600, and that's it. That covers hotel, food, drinks, and gambling."

Anthony—who, like a lot of casino regulars, prefers to remain anonymous—says that $600 might sound like a lot of money, but he can afford it. He's a stockbroker with an established list of clients. He doesn't have a mortgage or a family; the casino is his one vice.

"I know guys who go skiing every weekend with their wives and kids, and that'll set them back a grand, easily. It's just a matter of perception: some people look down on gambling and see it in a negative light, but for me it's just recreation, no different from a weekend on the slopes. Besides, sometimes I come home with more money than when I left; how many skiers can say that?"

Anthony first caught the casino bug about seven years ago, and ironically, it was a lottery that got him gambling.

"I bought a ticket from my nephew for a raffle that his hockey team was holding. First prize was a trip for two to Jamaica or some place like that. Second prize was a weekend trip to Reno. I won second prize—the tickets actually arrived on my birthday. I took my girlfriend at the time down with me: she stayed in the room watching movies, while I stayed down in the casino at the blackjack tables."

Anthony enjoyed his free trip so much that he started paying his own way to Las Vegas and Reno two or three times a year. He found that he had a knack for gambling, especially blackjack, but most of all, he enjoyed the glitter and hypnotic activity of the casinos—a stark contrast to the long hours in his dreary office.

"In a lot of ways it's like being involved in a really intense sporting competition. Your adrenaline gets running, your concentration is completely focused, it's like all your senses are heightened. I'm never going to be in the seventh game of a Stanley Cup final or anything like that, but I'll tell you, when I'm on a roll at the blackjack table or the roulette table, it's as exciting as anything I could imagine."

While Anthony enjoys most games the casino has to offer, he does play his favorites.

"I'll play slot machines every once in a while, but only when I have some spare change I want to get rid of. They don't do a lot for me because there's really no skill involved. Blackjack is more my style because if you take your time to learn the game and hone your skills, you can really improve your chance of winning. And I'm just starting to get the hang of baccarat—that's a whole other world. It's like something out of a James Bond movie."

Anthony's caught on to the fastest growing sector of the government-run gaming business. In many states and provinces, gaming revenues are outstripping lottery returns. In fact in Canada, casinos are one of the fastest growing industries. It's state-sanctioned gambling—code word "gaming"—and it's coming to a casino, lounge, and state fair near you.

The rise of gaming has been truly remarkable. In 1988, it was allowed in only two states: Nevada and New Jersey. Six years later, 23 states allowed gaming of one kind or another. Today, there is hardly a state or province that isn't on the game. Why? The simple answer is that there is no simple answer. During the 1980s and 1990s, Native groups across the continent began to take advantage of legal loopholes that allowed them to run casinos on their reserves. The success of these ventures probably served as an inspiration to governments looking to maintain levels of public services without obvious tax increases. The relative lack of resistance to the spread of lotteries also had an effect. Despite government fears, the public had embraced lotteries in a big way. Governments predicted—quite rightly—that gambling would be an even easier sell.

It all began quietly enough, and once again, Canada helped to lead the way. The dice got rolling in the early 1980s when some provinces and states started granting charity casino licenses. At the same time, some Native groups began running full-time casinos and bingo halls on their reserves. While both these ventures started off low-key, their success was unmistakable. Provincial governments were particularly impressed and concerned with the success of Native casinos near the Canada-U.S. border. Busloads of Canadians regularly trekked to these gambling halls to throw their money around; that was a lot of potential tax revenue heading south.

In December of 1989, the Manitoba government opened the $5 million Crystal Casino in Winnipeg's historic Fort Garry Hotel—the first permanent legal gambling house in the country, and one of the first modern casinos in North America outside of Las Vegas and Atlantic City. Despite its billing as a premier tourist attraction, the real purpose of the Crystal was to keep Manitoba's gamblers at home.

"There were charitable casinos throughout the province prior to the Crystal opening," says Susan Olyniuk of the Manitoba Lottery Commission. "A decision was made to close the charitable casinos and open this one, with all the revenue being earned from this one to go into specific health care projects in the province. This was done in agreement with the charitable groups."

The experiment was a success: in its first six months of operation, the Crystal Casino did almost $30 million worth of business, although the promised tourists never really showed up. Only 12 percent of the Crystal's customers over the two first two years came from outside of Manitoba, and three quarters of them were Winnipeggers. This is a typical scenario, says Dr. William Eadington, head of the Institute of Commercial Gaming at the University of Nevada. He says that while governments often make grand claims about the tourist appeal of casinos, the reality is very different.

"Adding a casino to a region does not necessarily stimulate the economy of that area," Dr. Eadington says. "The primary customers for most new casinos over the next decade in Canada and the U.S. will come from the region where the casino is located."

While Dr. Eadington agrees that casinos can help stop some money from leaving a province, it's not without cost.

"Consumers only have so much money to go around. Money spent at the casino is money that won't be spent in some other recreational area

CHEAT TO WIN

The sudden growth of gambling in Canada has created the perfect environment for casino cheats. Dealers are the first line of defense in a casino, and today, many of them are under-trained and overworked. Here are just some ways that naughty people try to get the upper hand at games of chance. Of course, we don't recommend that you try any of them.

Blackjack

If you wanted to cheat at blackjack, you could attend a blackjack seminar. By learning a card-counting system and betting strategies, you can significantly improve your chances at a blackjack table. In fact, it's hardly cheating, and although many casinos in Canada frown on counting, it's legal.

Another way to cheat at blackjack is to take over a table with a bunch of friends. During the first run through the deck, put tiny little bends and folds on the aces and face cards. The next time around, you will have a better idea of what cards the dealer is holding.

Roulette

One way of cheating at roulette is called "team past post"; one partner distracts the dealer by awkwardly trying to slip a large bet on the table after the ball has stopped. Meanwhile, the other partner deftly sneaks a large bet onto the table.

Another simpler, effective strategy at the roulette table is to argue

like restaurants, movie theatres, bowling alleys, bars, and other places where people spend discretionary income."

In other words, the government-subsidized casino monopolies are competing against other businesses in a local economy, businesses that can't afford the same built-in protection that a government can.

"Any community considering a casino should ask itself whether it would still want that casino if even one of the promised economic benefits did not materialize. If the answer is 'yes', then go ahead. But if the answer is 'no', you're making a great mistake by trying to exploit activities with the dealer. Claim that your chip was on the winning numbers, but someone else nudged it off, or come up with your own story. All you really want to do is waste the dealer's time. Time is money to a casino. A dealer is likely to pay you your measly ten bucks, rather than waste precious seconds. This strategy works best with small amounts of money.

Slot machines

There are a couple ways to beat the slots, but both of them involve you breaking the machine open. It's not as hard as it sounds.

A casino is usually a noisy, busy place, and an expert slot-cracker can get one open in seconds. The key is to create a diversion, and the two favorite kinds involve a man called a "blocker" and a woman called a "bloomer." The former is a great big guy who stands in front of a slot machine to block the casino staff's view while his accomplice breaks it open. The latter involves a woman, often scantily clad, who creates a diversion, by fighting with another "bloomer."

Once you break into a slot machine, you have two choices: you can simply scoop up as many coins as possible, or, if you're more sophisticated, reset the machine to give you a higher payoff than normal.

Craps

Craps are dice games, and have only recently become legal in Canada. There are two main ways to cheat at craps. The first involves fixed dice, which are weighted or shaved to land only on certain numbers. The other way is more difficult to master, but much more effective. It's called "the slide," and is a way of throwing the dice so that they spin around, creating the illusion of rolling without actually rolling. Only a very trained dealer can spot this kind of cheat.

that you don't like in an attempt to gain economic benefits that might not last in the long run."

Since Manitoba dealt its first hand in the casino business, other states and provinces quickly followed suit. In October 1993, Loto-Quebec completed almost $100 million worth of renovations to convert a building on Montreal's old Expo '67 site into a casino. Vancouver is also looking at a $750 million casino and convention complex. But not every province has found casinos to be the ticket to easy street. When Saskatchewan put two proposed casinos—one in Regina and the other in

Saskatoon—to a public vote, 75 percent of the voters said no to the idea. And in Nova Scotia, the public went nuts over the government's plan to build casinos in Halifax and Sydney: public opinion pollsters said that 60 percent of the population opposed the idea, while a group called People Against Casinos gathered almost 50,000 signatures on an anti-gambling petition. Meanwhile, southern states like Georgia and South Carolina, where the influence of fundamentalist Christian organizations is strong, have had a hard time winning support for gaming. (Or even lotteries, for that matter; Georgia, which joined the Multi State Lottery Association's Powerball team in 1995, dropped out of it two years later because of public pressure.)

The Windsor Casino appears to be everything the Ontario government had hoped for. Right now, it's annual gross revenues are close to half a billion dollars. And best of all, the Windsor Casino has turned out to be the tourist mecca that its operators—the government's partners in the venture include Las Vegas casino heavyweights Caesar's Palace and Circus Circus, along with Hilton Hotels—had hoped for. Eighty percent of the visitors are Americans, who cross the river to enjoy a cheaper dollar, tax-free winnings, and legal gambling.

"The Americans love it here," Anthony says. "You see them lined up around the block waiting to get in. It's a cheap holiday for them; what they save in air fare to Reno, they spend in the casino."

Even though he enjoys his gambling weekends, Anthony is not above the potential problems that casinos present. He says that problem gambling is an issue that governments should be aware of.

"I can see how casinos could be a problem for some people. I mean, there are people who practically live in the casino, and gamble away almost everything they've got. But these are people with a problem, and their problem won't go away if you close down the casinos. They'll find somewhere else to play, or they'll find some other addiction."

And is he concerned about the prospect of gambling attracting organized crime to Windsor?

"As far as I know, the government goes to great lengths to make sure that organized crime doesn't get involved in the casinos out here. But I'm sure it's like anything else; if there's enough money to be made at something, it's hard to police it one hundred percent."

In the final analysis, Anthony says, gambling should be accepted at its face value. "Look. It's recreation. It's something I do for fun. And just like anything else these days, it costs money to go to the casino. As long as you keep it in the proper perspective, and don't forget that it's supposed to be fun, I don't see how there could be a problem."

THE UPPER HAND

 Those benevolent folks who run casinos are not beyond every psychological trick in the book to keep you playing, and spending, longer. Here are just a few of the things your government does to keep you at the gaming tables.

- Men are often met at the door by beautiful women in skimpy out fits, offering them drinks. The idea is to get the old testosterone flowing, a sure-fire way of getting men to bet more.
- A lot of state-of-the-art casinos and bingo halls brag about their hi-tech air filtration systems. These were not installed, as opera- tors suggest, over concerns about second-hand smoke. Fresh air keeps players alert and awake, and more apt to gamble.
- Some casinos actually spray a chemical called Oderant 1, which is said to stimulate players to bet.
- Casinos are always dimly lit, to cut down on annoying and tiring glare.
- Slot machines pay fewer big jackpots than they used to; these days, though, they do pay out smaller amounts more frequently. That's because psychologists have found that such "intermittent rewards" are the most effective way to hook people on the slots.
- Casinos aim for a constant level of noise and activity, to create a hypnotic "land that time forgot." Casino players usually remem- ber the time the next day, when they realize how much money they've spent.

They are supposed to be the Next Big Thing in lotteries. In fact, they may just be the most devastating social problem the government has ever willingly unleashed on an unsuspecting public. They're called Video Lottery Terminals, VLTs for short. Their supporters claim that they will revolutionize the lottery business, adding hundreds of millions of dollars to state and provincial coffers virtually overnight, and with a revenue potential only limited by the number of machines in place.

These little, computerized bandits—which electronically simulate slot machines and popular poker card games—are also the most addictive form of betting ever invented, often referred to as the crack cocaine of the gambling world.

TIME IS MONEY

The more deals, spins, and pulls a casino can generate per hour, the more money it can make, and that's why the operators go to great lengths to ensure that both players and dealers, are operating at maximum warp speed.

How important is speed? Well, you probably thought all those video cameras set up in the casino were installed for security. That's part of the story, but what the operators really want to do is monitor their staff to make sure they're shuffling and dealing fast enough.

Here is the typical output per game per hour that casino operators look for:

- A slot machine: 350 pulls
- A roulette wheel: 45 spins
- A blackjack table: 75 games
- A craps table: 150 rolls

Calgary's Peter S. is one man whose life was ruined by VLT addiction.

"It's a basic story that's probably been told by hundreds of people," Peter says. "The government introduced the VLTs in Calgary in the bars about two years ago. I watched people playing them for a few weeks thinking, 'What a bunch of dummies wasting their money.' Then one day I saw a guy get a thousand bucks out of one of them. I hadn't realized that our VLTs were paying off like that."

Peter decided to try his luck. He started out playing a couple of dollars at a time; before he knew it, he was dropping 10, 20, 50 dollars at a time. It was unfamiliar territory for Peter. He'd never been much of a gambler before. Sure, he'd buy the occasional lottery ticket, and he'd been to the casino at the Calgary Stampede a couple of times, but that was the extent of it.

"The hook was the Big Win. You play a couple of bucks and lose a couple of bucks, that was nothing. It didn't really zing me until the first time I won $460. I'd been playing for about half an hour, and I thought to myself that was pretty good money."

Peter soon found himself slipping into the bar with four rolls of dollar coins in his pocket. With a ten-dollar maximum bet allowed in Alberta, those "loonies"—all 100 of them—wouldn't last long. He'd win the odd

No Honeymoon in Vegas

The people of Nevada—the heart of America's gambling industry—are ranked near the bottom when it comes to buying lottery tickets.

jackpot, and a couple times he recalls going home with $1,700 in his
pocket. But more than likely, he'd lose it all. One night, between seven
o'clock and midnight, he lost $1,100; even on a good night, he figured to
lose at least a couple hundred.

"Originally, I figured that I was going to win; I figured that my luck
can't be bad forever. Towards the end, after I had accumulated huge debts,
I was using the excuse that I have to get my money back. The last couple
of months I was just chasing my money, if you will. All I hoped was that
if I got even, I'd quit. And of course, I never come even close to winning.
Looking back now, trying to get my money back was just as good an
excuse as any. Just as long as I was playing—that's all that really mattered."

Soon, Peter's career started to suffer. He was an outside salesman for
a company that sold tools and equipment. It was a good job, but one that
unfortunately allowed him the kind of flexibility to nurture his addiction.

"I did most of my gambling during the day. I'd go into work in the
morning, and say that I was going out on calls, and head to the bar at ten
o'clock, come up with some lame excuse why I didn't come back to work
at lunch time, and be home at five o'clock. Everybody figured everything
was copacetic, because I wasn't going out at night. My problem wasn't
that evident at home."

It quickly became evident at work. His sales dropped, and he turned
to desperate measures in order to compensate.

"I started selling stock off cheap to guys, and instead of turning the
money into the company, I'd keep it, thinking that I was going to take
their fifty bucks, make three hundred, and give them their fifty back. Of
course, it never worked out that way. I just got myself further and further
into a hole, until finally they called me on it. I ended up losing my job in
mid-December. A seventeen-year career down the tubes."

Out of work two weeks before Christmas, with a wife and two children to support, Peter still managed to keep his habit up. He got a few
bank loans on the side, without telling his wife. But the house of cards col-
lapsed when he tried one scam too many.

"We did get a loan that my wife knew about, a consolidation loan to

HOWDY, STRANGER

New to gambling? Here's a thumbnail guide to what's going on at your local casino.

Baccarat
Game type: Exotic card game.
Object: To guess which of two hands will have a point total closest to nine.
Scoring: Cards are worth their face value.
Play: Dealer deals two hands of two cards, face down. One is called "the banker's hand," the other, "the player's hand." You bet on the hand you think will total closest to nine.
Tip: It's a simple game, but seems to have a rich, unspoken etiquette. Your best bet is to start out on mini-baccarat, the beginner's version of the game.

Blackjack
Game type: Poker-style card game.
Object: To get as close to 21 points as possible, without going over. You must beat the dealer.
Scoring: Aces equal 1 or 11 points; all face cards equal 10 points; all other cards are worth their face value.
Play: The dealer shuffles a number of decks together (usually six) then deals you two cards: one face up, the other face down. You can either take more cards ("draw") or pass on more cards ("stay" or "hold"). You can draw as many cards as you like as you try to get close to the magic 21, but if you go over, you automatically lose.

Keno
Game type: Casino lottery.
Object: To guess the numbers that will be selected in a random draw.
Play: You pick anywhere from one to 20 numbers on an 80 number ticket, and place a bet. Numbers are drawn to match, just like in a lottery.
Tip: Keno usually has by far the worst odds of any casino game.

pay off all our credit cards. Within a week of doing that, I went into one of the department stores and reopened my credit card account. I bought some gift certificates, then cashed them in for a ten dollar fee. In a matter

Pai Gow
Game type: Asian game, vaguely similar to baccarat, that uses dominos instead of cards.
Object: To score higher than the "banker" on both your hands.
Play: Each turn, a new player is designated banker. The dealer then deals each player a stack of dominos, which the players organize into two hands. You play against the banker, unless you're the banker, in which case, you play against everyone.
Tip: If you've never played before, just walk up to the pai gow table and hand everyone a $20 bill. Then leave. It'll save you a lot of time and money.

Roulette
Game type: Guessing game.
Object: To guess which of 38 numbers a little marble will land on.
Play: This game dates back to Roman times, when players used a numbered chariot wheel. The dealer spins a small wheel in one direction, then ships a marble around the hub of the wheel in the opposite direction. Players put their bet on a big, felt-covered table on numbers corresponding to numbers on the wheel.
Tip: Each of the numbers has color: either red or black. You're also allowed to bet on which color you think will come up, and that's what Chris does because there is a 50 percent chance of being right—your best odds in any casino game.

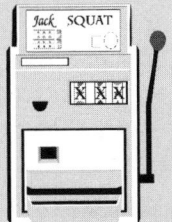 *Slot Machines*
Game type: Mechanical or hi-tech betting machines.
Object: Put money in slot. Win money.
Play: Put money in slot. Pull lever. Wait. Repeat. Repeat.
Tip: Slot machines offer many different games with numerous winning combinations. You won't care. Just put money in slot and pull.

of ten days, I racked up $2,300 charges on the card."

A little while later, the store called Peter's wife and questioned her about the new charges. Had the card had been lost or stolen? She con-

---

REALLY DUMB THINGS TO SAY IN THE CASINOS

- At the blackjack table. "I keep forgetting: are aces high or low?"
- At the slot machine. "I think something's wrong with this machine: my comb keeps getting stuck."
- At the pai gow table. "I'm new at this game, folks, so take it easy on me!"
- At the keno board. "Bingo!"
- At the roulette table. "Boy, that little white mint doesn't taste very good."
- At the baccarat table. "Damn! I knew I should have bet on the other hand!" (Note: repeat after every round.)
- To the casino bouncer. "This place is a rip-off! I want my money back now or I'm going to have to bust some heads!"

---

fronted Peter, and he admitted what he'd done.

"The worst part of it is that you're living a never-ending lie. You're cheating on your family, conniving, telling lies everywhere so you can get your time to gamble. Nothing else matters: your kids don't matter, your wife, your job. It's constant. You sit in front of the machine pushing the button, thinking about how you're going to get another hundred bucks so that tomorrow you can get the big win happening."

That credit card trick was the last straw for Peter's wife; she showed him the door.

Peter had hit rock bottom, and he knew it. He decided to get some help, but found very little available. And as for the government who owned and operated the VLTs? Back then, they offered no support system or programs for people who became addicted to these games. Finally, Peter's luck turned. He was admitted into the Walter Thorpe Recovery Center in Lloydminster, Alberta, as part of their first-ever treatment program for problem gamblers. Despite the severity of his addiction, Peter was optimistic from the start about his chances for recovery.

"The VLTs are kind of like a cocaine high; you're up quick and then down quick. If any good can be said about having a problem with the VLTs, it's usually a short amount of time, like a year, and the devastation is done. The foundation has only had a year to crack it, so it's easier to repair, whereas a longer term gambler faces a more gradual deterioration. It takes them a lot longer to patch things together and get things back on track."

VLTips

Still interested in trying your luck at VLTs? Well, how about this. The machines are rigged—excuse me, set—in such a way that makes it impossible for you to come out ahead on them. People who play the games, believing that they have a winning formula to beat the system, are fooling themselves, and what an expensive folly it is.

The kinds of VLT machines used by most lottery corporations in Canada are what are called "6/5" machines. That means that on a full house, they pay six-to-one on your bet—six dollars for every one dollar you bet—and on a flush, they pay five-to-one. The payout is poor, and these machines wouldn't last five seconds in Las Vegas—where "9/6" machines are the standard—or in Canada, for that matter, if governments didn't hold a monopoly on them.

If you still want to play VLTs, here are a few tips to help you minimize your losses:

1. Set a budget and stick to it. No, you're not going to hit the jackpot if you plug in just one more dollar.
2. Don't play regularly. Treat VLTs like any other form of entertainment, something you do every once and a while to relax, socialize, and have fun.
3. Don't make a habit of playing by yourself. It's supposed to be fun, remember? Hermits have fun by themselves, the rest of us need our friends around.
4. If you go to a casino that has VLTs, it might help a little to play the machines nearest to the main doors or in some other prominent place. Such high profile machines are sometimes set to pay out more often.
5. Repeat after me: "I can't beat the VLT. I can't beat the VLT." Very good!

After extensive treatment, Peter returned to his family and found a new job. Despite his bad experience with VLTs, Peter is not bitter towards the government. He says that he—and all problem gamblers—have to take responsibility for their own mistakes.

"I was talking to a guy who said, 'You know, if the government came out and said that it was going to raise the taxes of everyone in Alberta by ten dollars, there'd be a revolt. But you can sit in the bar watching people pump hundreds of dollars a night into the VLTs without batting an eye.'"

But Peter adds a word of caution. Are our governments, with an over-reliance on lottery revenue, treading down a path similar to the one that led to Peter's downfall? In a way, and in a very short time, governments have become hooked on VLTs just as surely as any compulsive gambler.

"Let's face it. VLTs are a government money-maker; they're here to stay. But let's keep the programs in place to help the casualties of the system. Because a certain percentage are going to be devastated by it. While all of us are responsible for our own actions, the government, by running the VLTs, has a responsibility to the people who play them."

CHAPTER 15

BUSINESS

Lotteries aren't just fun and games. They're business. Big business. In North America alone they bring in $30 billion, and around the world lotteries turn over $90 billion every year. While the lotteries are usually run by a bunch of overpaid, bureaucratic fat cats, the real heart and soul belongs to the ticket sellers, those dedicated men and women who, in return for practically nothing, ensure that you never miss your weekly—daily? hourly?—fix. These people are the forgotten heroes of the lotteries; people just like Vancouver's "Friendly" Glen Masson.

Glen started selling lottery tickets back in 1980, when he couldn't find any other work. Someone at the welfare office suggested Glen talk to the Kinsmen, a service club that in those days earned a little extra cash wholesaling tickets. The Kinsmen agreed to help Glen out, and gave him a bunch of tickets to sell—on credit.

"If it was today, I wouldn't have been able to go into business," Glen says. "Now you have to buy tickets directly from the government, and they're not about to extend credit to anyone."

To say that Glen started off modestly would be an understatement. His first establishment consisted of a card table and folding chair at the end of a supermarket parking lot.

"I worked in all kinds of weather; it'd be colder than a bugger out there. I had no machine at that time. Then a couple of the boys in the Super Valu took pity on me and built me a kiosk. Nothing fancy, just a tiny, open air booth with a little electric heater. I sure appreciated it, though."

BAD BUSINESS

Not every ticket seller is as honest as Friendly Glen. Just ask Arlington, Virginia's Ray Bernard. In May of 1997, Bernard bought a ticket on the state lottery at the Royal Lee Bar and Grill, playing the same set of numbers he'd played for three years. When he went in to get his ticket validated a few days later, he found out he didn't have a winner, but noticed that the big ticket had been sold in the deli. On closer inspection, he realized that the winning numbers—worth a cool $6.8 million—were his old favorites. Bernard called the police, who charged the store owner with doing the old switcheroo, slipping Bernard a useless ticket when he'd come to check his numbers. In the end, Bernard got his money, and the store owner got five years to practice his sleight-of-hand in the state slammer.

And thus, Friendly Glen's ticket kiosk was born. Safely tucked inside, Glen was able to get a BCLC computer to go on-line and sell tickets. "The computer belongs to the lottery corp. There's a meter on it that tells how much you've sold—of course, they know all that anyway. They know everything."

Glen worked long and hard for his modest income, for the life of the ticket seller is far from opulent. In British Columbia, sellers make five cents on every dollar, and contrary to public belief, there is no bonus awarded for selling a winning ticket.

"You don't get anything. That's a myth. The seller only gets what the winner feels like giving him. When they started up, things were different, because they had problems getting people to sell tickets, so there was this incentive; they gave you ten percent or something like that. You have to do a hell of a lot of business to make any money—oh man, do you ever!"

On a good week, Glen sold $300 worth of tickets, earning himself a less-than-princely $15. On a bad week—well, things got downright ugly.

"I'd keep the tickets at home in my damn dresser drawer, and only bring in what I needed to work. Some bugger knew what day the tickets were delivered—what day I took them home—and one day he broke into my place. He got the tickets plus some money I hadn't put into the bank, foolishly. That left me $13,000 out of pocket. That wasn't a very happy day, I can tell you."

YE OLDE LOTTO SHOPPE

Here's Friendly Glen Masson's advice for anyone interested in starting their lottery ticket kiosk:
1. Try to get a spot indoors.
2. Look after your money. Put it in the bank every night.
3. Don't give any credit.
"There's no trouble becoming a retailer if you've got the place to sell. But things are harder now than when I started out. If you're going to open on a shoestring like I did, you can't just set up a card table somewhere."

But Glen's business took a turn for the better in the spring of 1988. He and his partner Ron Davis had sent away to Ontario to get a book on wheeling systems. The idea was to make a little extra selling the book in the kiosk. They figured, what the heck, why not try the system out?

"The book contained about twenty different systems; we picked the one that cost $18, then stuck up a sign that said, 'Try our system.'"

Along came Lewis Burke. The real-estate marketing executive was out doing some shopping when he saw Friendly Glen's sign. "First he asked us to explain our system, but when we started he said, 'Oh no, no, no—it's all a bunch of numbers. I hate numbers. What's it cost?'"

Glen told him the price, and Burke, who'd never played the lottery before, threw $18 across the counter, and said, "Here's my business card. You guys pick the numbers for me. Call me if it wins; don't bother if it doesn't. If I do win, ten percent is yours."

That night, Glen, Ron, and another friend went to their favorite café for dinner and to pick Lewis Burke's numbers.

"The three of us just yelled out numbers, and I'd write them down as they were called out. I mean, we had no secret system."

That was a Saturday. On Sunday morning, Glen went in to work to check tickets on the computer. First, he tried his own. No winner. So then he tried Burke's tickets. The computer hummed for a second, then a message appeared on the small screen: BE AT LOTTERY BRANCH AT RICHMOND TOMORROW MORNING. YOU HAVE JUST WON $3.6 MILLION.

Thanks to the wheeling system, the lucky numbers hit on a number of smaller prizes as well. Burke's final take: $3,788,659. Glen grabbed Burke's card and phoned him.

"I got his answering machine because he was at church. So I left a message. Well, of course, he just thought it was a bunch of b.s.; I'm sure I would have, too."

Through the course of the day, Glen and Ron tried to get through to Burke. Finally Ron reached him. He thought Ron was kidding. "I'm dead serious. you're a millionaire," Ron said.

There was silence on the end of the phone, and Ron thought something had happened to the poor man. When he finally spoke, he couldn't believe his good luck.

"We told him, the first thing you do is change your telephone number," Glen recalls. "Be down here Monday with your lawyer, we'll have a car waiting."

The next day, Burke picked up his winning ticket, and took the limousine for the short trip to Richmond to collect his check. Glen and Ron went along for the ride. Nobody was prepared for the flood of interest in this story.

"When we got to the lottery office, there were quite a few fellows from the press, and they were saying how we could have easily taken Burke's ticket, put it in our envelope, and put our ticket into his envelope. Did that cross ever cross our minds? Well, not until the press got hold of us."

Burke was suitably impressed with Glen's honesty. "I am a very lucky and very grateful man," he told reporters assembled at the lottery office. "They've made me a millionaire when they could have claimed the ticket for themselves. They're good people."

Burke truly was grateful, and true to his word, he showed up at Friendly Glen's later that day with three $125,000 checks for the three men who picked his winning numbers.

"We did a hell of a lot of business that week. It hit the front page of the newspaper and they had a great big picture of me in a pink T-shirt with "It Pays to Shop at Friendly Glen's" across the back. We were swamped for a while. But how soon people forget! You have to churn out a millionaire a week to keep them interested, I guess."

While $125,000 might not sound like a fortune, it was more money than Glen had ever seen, so he decided to put it to work for him. He bought half a duplex, and went into business with his friend, Doris Colligan.

"The duplex had a two-car garage in it, so we tore that out and put in some carpet and painted the walls and put in an office. I bought a couple of computers and a fax machine, everything you need nowadays. So we're running a mom and pop bookkeeping agency, called Friendly Glen's

Bookkeeping. It's going really well; Doris does all the work, and she's swamped. I'm just the gopher; I go to the bank and here and there."

At the time of his interview, Glen said that he didn't have much left from his windfall—there was about $5,000 in the bank—but that didn't bother him. He had a place to live and a steady income, and wound up better off on the business side of the luck of the draw.

When it comes to Canadian politics, lotteries and scandal seem to go hand in hand. In the mid-1980s, Ontario was rocked with the news that half a dozen people given plum jobs at the lottery corporation were friends or relatives of prominent Conservative politicians. Then there was Manitoba's Manness Madness, which saw a lease for the province's rural VLT headquarters granted without tender to a supporter of the Finance Minister, Clayton Manness.

Cronyism is one problem. But the distribution of lottery profits has also caused a few headaches. Today, most provinces avoid hassles and just stick the money in general revenue. But in the good old days, most provinces earmarked lotto loot for specific programs . . . which led to some rather oddball awards.

In Ontario, for example, Wintario profits were targeted for public-access recreation and culture programs. But as the 1977 fiscal year came to a close, the lottery corporation found itself with three times the money they'd planned on, and got a little desperate in attempts to dole it out. Here's just a sampling of how the voluntary tax money was spent:

• An exclusive Belleville golf club received $200,000 to rebuild its fire-ravaged clubhouse. In fact, the clubhouse was already fixed, and the money went to fix up the tennis courts and swimming pool.

• Greenhills Funland Incorporated, owners of a semi-private golf course near London, got $166,000 to build a semi-private, 18-hole golf course.

• An old age home in Kingston got a brand new wheelchair bus, but faced some heavy restrictions. Since Wintario money was tagged for recreation and culture only, the seniors could use the bus to go bowling or to the opera, but not to go to the hospital.

Every province has had its share of backroom dealing. But try as they might, no province comes close to British Columbia. In terms of scope, audacity, and sheer numbers, the Left Coast has earned a coveted spot in our hall of fame as the Lotto Scam Capital of Canada. Here's just a taste of what British Columbians have had to put up with:

• The wife of Education Minister Pat McGeer wasn't happy with the

$20,000 research grant she was offered in January of 1979. The reason? She wanted more. "I'd asked for $45,000, and the project is budgeted very tightly," Edith McGeer, a respected neuro-chemical researcher, told the press at the time. Mr. and Mrs. McGeer did not believe that the grant, as disappointing as it was, constituted a conflict-of-interest.

• In the first six months of 1981, Social Credit ridings received 84 percent of all lottery funds, prompting complaints by the Ombudsman. Coincidentally, the Socreds, with 54 percent of the seats in the provincial legislature, were in power.

• In the spring of that same year, Tourism Minister and Provincial Secretary Bill Reid, who was also in charge of B.C.'s lottery grant program, gave a $277,065 grant to a company owned by his campaign manager and another friend. Reid later quit over the scandal, and would be sued by the government for part of the money. The parties eventually settled out of court. A review of grants by the provincial Ombudsman less than a year after Reid's tenure revealed that one in four grants broke the government's own rules.

• In the summer of 1990, a school in North Peace River, home riding of Education Minister Tony Brummet, got a $63,000 grant to build a track and field facility—even though the government guidelines clearly excluded schools from receiving lottery funds.

• In that same year, Provincial Secretary Howard Dirks (B.C. went through a lot of Provincial Secretaries in those days) okayed 23 grants worth $1.1 million—a sizeable chunk of the lottery fund—to groups in his home riding. Some of the money went to a polygamous community whose leader reportedly told his 300 followers to vote for Dirks.

• And finally, there's the story of the Celebrated Jumping Frog of Castlegar County. In 1979, Travis Green—the Canadian Frog Jumping Champion, Junior Division—and his owner Jim Chapman were given $250 to attend the world championships. The grant caused a lot of controversy, and left Chapman . . . well, hopping mad. "I'm getting a lot of static," Chapman said at the time. "I don't think frog jumping is a sport. But I thought this would be fun for the kids."

In the old days, when North America first faced the reality of legal lotteries, people actually worried about questions of ethics and morals. Was it proper, morally speaking, for the government to condone and encourage gambling? Would lotteries erode the work ethic?

Quaint as these questions sound today, people were once seriously concerned about the social costs of lotteries. Thirty years later, the debate is all but forgotten. Almost everyone has tried their hand at some form of

LIFESTYLES OF THE RICH AND UNEMPLOYED

Can a million-dollar winner of a lottery collect unemployment insurance? You bet, according to Revenue Canada. Take the case of Maurice Diotte. In the summer of 1984, Windsor's Diotte was laid off from his job as a draftsman, and went on U.I. A few weeks later, he collected $1.2 million in a Lottario draw. Despite his good fortune, he continued to collect unemployment benefits for almost a year.

"I paid into it for twenty years," Diotte told a reporter for the *Montreal Gazette* at the time. "These are my benefits and I'm entitled to them."

Revenue Canada agreed. Lottery winnings, along with inheritances, do not affect a person's eligibility for U.I. So if Lady Luck comes knocking on your door, quit your job—and apply for unemployment insurance right away.

However, lottery players in Florida may not be so lucky. Under proposed legislation in that state, welfare recipients who win on the lottery might have to pay back a share of their loot. Under the plan, anyone who wins $100,000 or more could lose up to half their winnings to cover previous welfare payments. In 1998, 70 Florida welfare recipients won more than $100,000 on the state lottery; 40 of those were big jackpot winners.

"Public assistance is not an entitlement," a supporter of the bill told the press. "It's a two-way street."

Good point. But does that mean that when you don't win the lottery the government will refund your ticket costs? Or is it one of those two-way streets that just goes one way?

legalized gambling, and yet no city has ever turned into Sodom or Gomorrah.

The weakness of the morality debate was that the anti-lottery camp never defined what "immoral" behavior was. They put forth vague religious arguments—the first line of attack in lieu of real evidence—but never clearly said what their beef was. Looking back, though, they had two particular worries: that lotteries would encourage some people to become problem gamblers, and that these games would put a financial burden on those who could least afford it, the poor.

Today, it's hard for everyday folks to figure out if concerns were legit-

INVESTED INTERESTS

 Not content with T-bills or pork futures, one Australian investment group decided to add the Virginia state lottery to it's portfolio. Their strategy was simple and straightforward; they planned a hostile take-over of all seven million tickets in the February 1992 draw. Time was not on their side, however, and when the bell rang to end sales on the draw, the Aussies had acquired only five million tickets.

Still, as majority shareholder, they managed to wrest control of the jackpot away from other players, and won themselves the top prize: a $1.3 million annual dividend for the next 20 years.

imate. Your government lottery corporations are cavernous and dark, and like to keep their little secrets to themselves; they don't allow everyday folks to review their records. You should take any reports or studies they release with a few grains, if not an entire shaker, of salt. Having said that, there's no evidence that the Big Game and Powerball have created a continent of problem gamblers. In fact, hard core gamblers avoid lotteries for the same reason the rest of us should: the odds are terrible. And when we contacted several Gamblers' Anonymous branches, including the one in that lottery hotbed, Montreal, they said that currently they saw very few "problem" lottery players.

However, with newer forms of "lotteries" like casinos and VLTs, your friendly, neighborhood lotto corporations are in question. They've become, in effect, playground pushers, taking advantage of the highly addictive nature of these games in a never-ending pursuit of pure profit.

As to the second concern, lotto types take great pains to point out that, according to their studies (shake, shake, shake), lotteries don't hurt the poor. The statistics prove that poor people don't play lotteries any more than middle class or rich people. Well . . . yes, but this distorts the truth. While the percent of poor and rich who buy lottery tickets is roughly the same, poor people tend to spend a bigger proportion of their available income on tickets. Two private sector studies found lotteries to be a regressive form of tax—the most regressive form, after cigarettes and alcohol—which means that poor people spent a lot more of their spare

---

"STAT" OF THE UNION

 Don't believe everything you read, especially when it comes to state lotteries. In 1997, a group of San Antonio, Texas college students discovered that the stats posted by the state lottery were not entirely above board.

An ad for Cash 5 claimed that there were more than 60,000 winners each week on the game. But the students took a closer look and found that the average number of winners never exceeded 57,500, and some weeks, the number of winners was well below 50,000.

---

cash on lottos than others, but benefited less from the proceeds of lottery profits. For example, a 1996 study of the Virginia lottery found that 61 percent of the tickets were sold to a mere eight percent of the population, and that 16 percent of those big players earned less than $15,000 a year. Like Robin Hood gone bad, lotteries take from the poor and give to the rich.

Our biggest beef with lotteries has nothing to do with the intrinsic morality of them, but in the clearly amoral way they play the game. Lottery corporations tend to forget that they are government agencies— of, for, and by the people—and that consequently they must take extra care to treat their customers, (i.e., owners) with honesty and dignity. So are lotteries immoral? It's hard to say. But they're certainly not above reproach, and definitely not beyond serious, thoughtful discussion.

CHAPTER 16

WHAT THE FUTURE HOLDS

If you thought the first 40 years of lottomania were something, wait until you see what's in store. Now that lotteries and gambling have become acceptable—respectable, even—governments can focus all their attention on improving and upgrading the gaming industry. On top of that, online technologies are changing the game faces.

Greg Ziemack is one man who keeps focused on the future of lotteries. Ziemack is president of the North American Association of State and Provincial Lotteries, a voluntary organization that helps individual lottery companies stay in touch and keep pace with trends in the industry. He says that it's an interesting time for lotteries; on the one hand, the industry has experienced a lot of growth over the last ten years. On the other, lotteries are now facing a tremendous challenge from casinos and other forms of legalized gambling, and at the same time, are finding themselves increasingly under the public microscope.

"Public opinion of lotteries is still very positive," Ziemack says. "Of the thirty-eight U.S. lotteries, twenty-three were voted in by referendum, where people actually had a vote. But in 1988, in the U.S., the Indian Gaming and Regulation Act was passed, which allowed Native Americans to own high-stakes bingos and casinos, resulting in more and more casinos being built; the act also permitted states to allow private interest casinos to be built. As a result of the mushrooming private interest casinos, the whole industry has come under great scrutiny; the critics of gaming have formed together and have become more vocal."

While public support remains strong, it's a lot harder for lotteries to get up and running. In the mid-1990s, lottery referendums in Oklahoma and Alabama were defeated, while the U.S. federal government set up a national gaming commission to examine the issue. It released its findings in June 1999, and although critical of lotteries, it failed to make an impression on the public imagination. But lotteries have been affected more by casino competition than political perceptions.

"The casino industry has definitely affected the lottery industry," Ziemack says. "Lotteries used to experience double-digit growth, particularly in the 1970s and 1980s. But the last five years has seen single digit growth, and the last two years some lotteries have actually experienced a drop in sales. But in many ways, the competition has been a good thing. The multi-state lotteries with their huge jackpots have been very successful, but that may have brought a bit of nonchalance to the industry. Now, when a jackpot gets to be $50 or $60 million, players just don't get as excited as they used to. Many people won't play until it gets to $100 million."

While public tastes and policies change, technology may have the biggest influence over the future of lotteries. Computers and the Internet have already had a large impact. In fact, the first wave of lottery growth was spurred by the introduction of computerized ticketing systems in the 1970s. Today, the choices are growing. Already, Europeans are tinkering with something called a "smart card," a kind of lottery credit card with a built-in computer chip. The card will keep track of your ticket numbers, tell you if you've won, and key you into VLT and other hi-tech games. The best part—or worst, depending on how much you value your privacy—is that the smart card will automatically take your expenses out of your bank account, and deposit your winnings into it.

Of course, the Internet is proving to be a breeding ground for lottery and gambling companies and services. There are virtual casinos, lottery-style games that offer service in multiple languages, and hundreds of links to lottery games around the world. What hasn't happened yet is one of the major lottery players getting into the Internet in a big way. Part of the concern is that governments haven't figured out how to regulate the technology and use it safely.

"I think people should approach Internet gaming with caution," says Ziemack. "There are something like six hundred illegal gaming sites on-line right now. As it stands, in the U.S. there are no lotteries on the Internet. Right now, there are two proposed laws being looked at. Both of them would make it illegal to play Internet lotteries from the home, while allowing some forms of parimutuel betting—on things like greyhound racing, horse racing, and jai alai. So, it's hard to tell where all this will wind up. It seems clear, though, that in the long run the Internet will have a big effect on lottery sales."

There are signs that the lotteries and legalized gambling have peaked. Since the mid-1990s, lottery sales have steadily increased, but the profitability of state and provincial lottery companies has waned. In 1992, 40 cents of every lottery dollar went into government pockets; four years later, it was down to 33 cents. Today, the average net profits are even lower, and lottery watchers believe that prize payouts and overhead will continue to grow in the lottery business. And far from a salvation, the growth of legal gaming suggests desperation on the part of lawmakers. Gambling is much less profitable than lotteries, much harder to police, more expensive to administer, and more open to abuse and corruption. States are also in the difficult position of competing against themselves. Casinos and other gambling venues take money out of the lotteries' pockets, and force states to throw an ever-increasing percentage of their earnings into the prize pool to keep the public's interest.

One of the more recent developments is the growing private sector creeping into the lottery business. In England five years ago, a private consortium called Camelot won a contract to run the first national lottery that country had seen in 150 years. Camelot's shareholders include Virgin Records founder Richard Branson, Cadbury Schweppes, makers of chocolates and ginger ale, and GTech, an American lottery company. Camelot quickly became one of the most successful lottery stories of all time. Within a week of its introduction in November of 1994, sales reached almost $100 million. The sales forecast for the first year was around $6 billion; Camelot exceeded that by almost $3 billion. Of course, Camelot was not without its problems. In the early days, the British tabloids had a field day with tales of hard luck lottery winners and scandals revolving around the distribution of lottery money. More significantly, a rift quickly formed between Richard Branson and the other major shareholder, GTech. Branson even went so far as to accuse the American lottery company of trying to bribe him, an allegation which was upheld in British court. Despite the problems, Camelot is a money-making machine for both government and its investors, and proves that the private sector has a place in the world of lotteries. In fact, the Camelot experience has been so successful that there's talk of spreading to other countries like Bermuda. It's an unprecedented move—no country has ever moved into another's lottery jurisdiction—and one that raises the spectre of a future haunted by large-scale, international lotteries.

YOU'RE THE TOPS:
BEST LOTTERIES AROUND THE WORLD

The Whole World Lottery Guide ranks Canada's Lotto 6/49 as one of the top lottery games in the world, while Australia—with four spots in the top ten—seems to be the haven for hardcore lottery players. Here is the guide's complete top ten, based on prize structures, odds, and taxation issues:

1. Australia's Ox Lotto
2. Australia's New South Wales Lotto
3. Canada's Lotto 6/49
4. Loto France
5. Germany's 6/49
6. UK's National Lottery
7. Australia's Powerball
8. Saturday Lotto 6/45, also from Australia
9. Hong Kong's Mark Six
10. The Netherlands' Lotto Jackpot

In total, Canada placed six lottos in the top 50—including Super 7, BC/49, and Lottario. The highest ranking U.S. lottery was the Daily Millions, at 17. Powerball and The Big Game both finished near the bottom of the list, largely because of the extremely high odds and less favorable tax status.

"The Internet has shrunken the world, so these new on-line technologies make it possible for one country to take its lottery across borders," says Ziemack. "I know that Australia has already discussed this idea somewhat. There's also a world lottery association looking at these issues closely. They're trying to develop guidelines to stop one country from impinging on another's territory. When we talk about the future, this is really going to be a big issue."

Over the last ten years, much of the growth in the lottery industry came as governments identified and targeted previously untapped markets. The growth in sports-based betting is a good example; games like sports lotteries attracted a young, male audience, many of whom rarely played traditional lotteries. However, as much as the provinces and states would like to repeat that kind of success, Ziemack does not expect to see many new markets breaking through.

"I think we're seeing the markets leveling off. I think expansion, if it comes, will be in the form of efficiency and technologies, as opposed to new markets being uncovered. There's a chance a handful of the thirteen states that don't already have lotteries might opt in—Arkansas and Hawaii, for example—but other than that, we've pretty much reached every segment we can, so now we're entering a mature phase of operations."

Market growth has peaked, but that's not necessarily bad news for the most important people in the lottery game: the players. Greater competition has forced lottery companies to become more sensitive to the needs of their players and make the games more attractive.

"Competition has been good for the players, and at the same time players have been getting more sophisticated," Ziemack says. "People now have so many choices, and they're used to having these choices. It's all part of the way society and business is going: we're becoming more and more a service culture, and that, in the end, is going to benefit players."